Frictions

Frictions: Inquiries into Cybernetic Thinking and Its Attempts towards Mate[real]ization

Edited by Diego Gómez-Venegas

meson press

The publication of this work was supported by the Open Access Publication Fund of Humboldt-Universität zu Berlin.

**Bibliographical Information of the
German National Library**
The German National Library lists this publication in the
Deutsche Nationalbibliografie (German National Bib-
liography); detailed bibliographic information is available
online at https://dnb.dnb.de

Published 2023 by meson press, Lüneburg.
www.meson.press

Design concept: Torsten Köchlin, Silke Krieg
Cover art: Diego Gómez-Venegas
Copy editing: Rowan Coupland
The print edition of this book is printed by Lightning Source,
Milton Keynes, United Kingdom

ISBN (Print):   978-3-95796-216-4
ISBN (PDF):   978-3-95796-217-1
DOI: 10.14619/2164

The digital editions of this publication can be downloaded
freely at: www.meson.press

Contents

Introduction: Cybernetic Thinking and Its Frictions

Diego Gómez-Venegas

The research interests and energies that initiated and then pushed the work that is now materialized in this volume are based on two main hypotheses. First, that by transcending the classic cybernetic epoch—i.e., going beyond the historical margins that have been used to frame it (Kline 2015, 4–6; Medina 2011, 20–24; Hörl and Hagner 2008; Pias 2004; Pickering 2002)—a somehow silent epistemic flow has moved from that field towards our present, becoming deeply entangled with contemporary net-worked societies. Many times discernible in the drive and visions of outcast scientists and short-lived projects, this flow, as well as its resonances, is what is here called *cybernetic thinking*. Second, it is by studying the *frictions* that may have determined the trajec-tories of such a flow—either its advances, setbacks, or changes of course—that we will be able to fully grasp the character and scope of this *cybernetic thinking*.

Therein lies the central premise of this book: the understanding that, as it were, epistemological progress is in effect the pro-duct of a series of frustrating, and sometimes even annoying, tug of war maneuvers. Put differently, the influence this epoch's underlying knowledge may have in the current state of affairs does not obey simple acts of epistemic concatenation, not even to distributed yet smooth chains of diffusion. Rather, this premise contends that in every single point of contact of those processes of concatenation and diffusion, a deep epistemological battle is held; one that has occasionally become visible through somehow thwarted attempts of implementation, where *the symbolic* theories sustaining this *cybernetic thinking* confront the real materiality that promises to concretize its application (Kittler [1989/1993] 1997; Ernst 2018). Still in other words, beyond a space of dispersion (Foucault 1972, 9–10), this *frictions*-focused inquiry signals a networked space of epistemic exchange where the operations taking place in its nodes are essential to trace the course of such a transfer, and, moreover, to grasp the constitution, even the transformation, of the episteme thus exchanged.

In order to assess these hypotheses, as well as the underlying premise connecting them, a lecture series on *Applied Cybernetics* was organized in Berlin between late-2019 and early-2020.[1] Focusing primarily on questions of implementation attempts and failure, the organization of this forum stressed the necessity that each of the five presentations were derived from distinct case studies—after all, the ethos of the Berlin school of media studies behind this initiative suggested that every insight was informed by the examination of concrete technological materialities. It was precisely this approach that first emphasized the role of *frictions* in this landscape. It seemed to be clear then that the historical role of cybernetics could not simply be explained by the success or failure of the projects that comprised it, but, alternatively, that such a dichotomy contained in itself epistemological potential. It was as if these case studies and their materialities pointed out, as it were, dialectical operations within which a fundamental *thing* was produced or rather harbored (Žižek, Ruda, and Hamza 2022, 9). That is to say that the scope of cybernetics could not merely be measured by the positive or negative outcomes of the projects drawing its topology. In a word, the *frictions* between this positivity and negativity showed essential aspects of the underlying episteme of cybernetics, signaling, moreover, the vectors

1   Conceived and coordinated by the author, this lecture series was supported and organized by the chair of media theories at the Institute of Musicology and Media Sciences of the Humboldt-Universität zu Berlin (HU), and the chair of literature and science at the Institute of Philosophy, Literary Studies, History of Science and Technology of the Technische Universität Berlin (TU). It took place at HU's Media Theater and in the Einstein Center Digital Future between November 13, 2019 and February 5, 2020 (Humboldt-Universität zu Berlin n.d.).

such an epistemological instantiation would be prone to follow afterwards.

At the same time however, this lecture series showed that this frictional condition of *cybernetic thinking* could be also revealed by media-historical analyses. In addition to the study of actual media technologies, presentations in this forum proved that research based on the documentation produced by some of these case studies, spoke too of struggles that nonetheless remained latent, or even active resonances in the historical account of cybernetics. It then became evident that, at a methodological level, there was a second order of *frictions*. Whereas one perspective investigated *cybernetic thinking* from the depths of machines, the other did so by tracing historical records. Even if their research paths seemed conflicting at first—the first moving, as it were, vertically, and the other horizontally—their crossing appeared not only complementary but particularly productive. Accordingly, the notion of *frictions* revealed itself as twofold: on one hand an object of research, on the other a method of inquiry. Could such an approach help to reinvigorate the attention that German media studies has paid to cybernetics for decades (Müggenburg 2017)? Would this perspective offer new insights into the historical and epistemological scope of cybernetics? Moreover, if so, to what extent would this enterprise help in tracing, and thus untangling, the relations between the classic cybernetic epoch and contemporary networked societies?

Convinced of the promising scope of these questions, in late 2020 I decided to transform them into a collective book project. More researchers joined this initiative and one year later things were moving forward. Now, after long hours have been invested in writing, discussing, and editing, readers can get involved in this effort too. In addition to this introduction they will find eight chapters that shed light on the relevance of *cybernetic thinking*, and, in doing so, they will also clarify how the question of *frictions* plays a role in such a discussion. First, a translation of Eva Schauerte's *"From Delphi to ORAKEL"* is offered. Beginning the book in this way is important in order to, as it were, contribute to paying off a still significant debt: sharing with a broader readership the robust body of work that within German media studies has traced the relevance of cybernetics, outlining what here is called *cybernetic thinking*. More importantly however, Schauerte's chapter shows us how this question may have played a role in the social consolidation of West Germany's democracy during the early 1970s. Paying attention to the work of systems theorist Helmut Krauch, Schauerte discusses the TV show *ORAKEL*; a political debate program broadcast by West Germany's public television of which Krauch was the mastermind. Implemented to strengthen socio-political deliberation, Schauerte stresses the role that telecommunications and computing technologies played in providing audiences *with real-time* participation in the political discussions held on this TV program. More substantially however, the author discusses how technological and political *frictions*—the lack of proper equipment, as well as pressures from the government—at the same time affected and shaped the character of this broadcast endeavor.

Moving forward, the following seven chapters are all original contributions to this volume. Chapter three is Isabell Schrickel's *"From Cybernetics to Sustainability."* There, the author presents part of her research on the work developed at the International Institute for Applied Systems Analysis (IIASA) during the 1970s and 1980s. Schrickel shows how the establishment of this institute in Austria not only expanded the discourse of cybernetics to new fields of inquiry and complexity, but also how IIASA operated as an actual hinge of scientific diplomacy between the East and West during some of the hardest years of the Cold War. Furthermore, Schrickel's chapter demonstrates that this context constituted a space of *friction*, where cybernetics was in effect challenged in the face of problems whose increasing complexity, it was then argued, surpassed the analytic capacities of this "old" science. In this sense, by properly emphasizing the historical prevalence of systems theories and systems thinking over cybernetics, we are

not only reminded of the long-standing and mutually beneficial
relations between these two fields, but of the inherent *frictions* underlying such a relation. Nevertheless, following the author we can see IIASA as a nodal point where cybernetics is not necessarily suppressed, but somehow transformed—if not also absorbed—and thus deviated.

Then, Sebastian Vehlken presents *"Social Supercolliders."* Focused on the *FuturICT* project, the author discusses the traces of this never-implemented initiative. One of the leading proposals within a colossal founding scheme of the European Union in the late 2000s, *FuturICT* aimed at becoming a technological "social supercollider" that promised to handle issues of high complexity both at European and global levels. Then, analyzing white papers, scientific articles, academic lectures, and a myriad of additional documents which *FuturICT* left behind, Vehlken critically discusses how the scientific discourse embedded in the project echoed cybernetics, thus constituting an instantiation of the *cybernetic thinking* this volume traces. More importantly, however, the author also examines and disentangles key arguments behind this proposal, showing how it remained stubbornly at odds with other contemporary approaches to social complexity. The main point of friction here, Vehlken shows, lay with *FuturICT*'s certainty that contemporary media technologies were able to model reality in all its complexity. Accordingly, the author formulates an argument which demonstrates that this sort of undertaking should have faced, regardless of whether it was implemented, an ethical dilemma: that transforming human social deliberation into a subject matter of complex technological models inevitably entailed leaving one of the components of that complexity out of the model.

Chapter five is my own contribution to this volume. Under the title *"Encoding from/to the Real,"* it returns to Chile's Project Cybersyn in order to media-archaeologically assess this case. By analyzing archival material that had so far remained undiscussed in the context of this seminal project, the chapter outlines a shift regarding its historical and epistemological relevance. In brief, the underlying thesis is that the emphasis on Stafford Beer's Viable System Model (VSM) as a mainly managerial technique of decision and control—most of the time exemplified by Cybersyn's compelling *"Opsroom"*—must be contrasted with the actual materialities and technologies through which the project was implemented. This leads, as shown in the chapter, to understanding Project Cybersyn as a system of information whose techno-epistemological core lies in the telecommunications network and processing unit that comprised it, rather than in its better-known operations room. Put differently, the cybernetic relevance of the case is found in circuits drawn by encoding protocols, telex networks, mainframe computers, and forecasting programs. Consequently, it is finally contended that these very circuits bring about a reorganization of the relations between the actors involved in them; a reorganization that, by constituting a media-genealogical horizon, delineates Project Cybersyn's contemporary scope.

The book continues with Wolfgang Ernst's chapter *"On the Notions of Cybernetic Frictions and its Role in Radical Media Archaeology."* As the title suggests, the author offers a programmatic formulation on the modes of inquiry into the legacy of cybernetics, and into the technological manifestations of such an inheritance. By properly reviewing cases in the realms of cybernetics, architecture, and the electric modeling of ecological systems, Ernst emphasizes the role played by implementation struggles in the development of cybernetics as a field of research, and in its consolidation as a proper science. The author contends that there were immanent *frictions* between the theories and models produced during the classic epoch of cybernetics, and the technological materiality then available—paraphrasing Ernst, the technology of the time was not sufficient to concretize those theoretical formulations. However, even if these *frictions* between models and technology seem to persist over time—although today in a smoother fashion—so too does the techno-logical

impetus for implementation: this becomes evident in the current   **13**
modeling of atmospheric and climate phenomena, but even
more transparently, Ernst argues, in earlier examples such as the
electric-circuit models of ecological and social systems developed by H. T. Odum and his team. In other words, the legacy
of cybernetics would keep moving over time and across fields
through this implementation drive which is expressed in actual
technological materiality—or in other words, through the *frictions*
there enclosed.

Chapter seven is Stefan Höltgen and Rolf F. Nohr's *"Teaching
Machines: Learning as Subjective Technique and Feedback Loop."*
Drawing on the history of teaching machines and their inception
in the 1950s, the authors trace the similarities and differences
between their instantiations in the United States and West Germany. More substantially however, Höltgen and Nohr focus their
study on the research and developments produced at Helmar
Frank's Institute for Cybernetics during the 1960s and early
1970s, showing precisely how the teaching machines they built
constitute proper examples of what here is called *cybernetic
thinking*. Providing an accurate recounting of the different types
of machines Frank's team were able to produce, the authors
reveal the techno-scientific discourse that shaped a mode of
understanding education, thus uncovering the social relation
between humans, knowledge, and machines which the Institute
for Cybernetics promoted. Even if the very progress of computing
made these machines obsolete, Höltgen and Nohr contend that
the open logic they entailed—students had to learn with them by
understanding their operations from within—teaches interesting
lessons. Opposing the closed architecture of the personal
computers that predominated from the late 1970s onwards, this
chapter asserts that current initiatives on open hardware would
emerge as contemporary inheritors of the approach developed at
West Germany's Institute for Cybernetics.

The eighth contribution is Thomas Fischer and Andrei Cretu's
chapter *"The Ashby Box: A Contextualization and Speculative*

14 *Remake.*" There, they present a thorough analysis of one of Ross Ashby's conceptual, yet operational machines. By deploying a genealogical account of this type of system, Fischer and Cretu draw a topology where, from the Turing Machine to Heinz von Foerster's theoretical notion of non-trivial machines, the electro-mechanical devices designed and built by Ashby play a fundamental role. In particular, the authors' work focuses on a later machine the British cybernetician developed at von Foerster's Biological Computer Laboratory during the 1960s. Called precisely the *Ashby Box*, this machine was not only used to teach engineering students foundational concepts of cybernetics, but, more substantially, it was itself a complex black box. Fischer and Cretu argue that while the Turing Machine relates to deductive reasoning, the Ashby Box operated in the realm of inductive reasoning, constituting an epistemological object that challenged students on the limits of undecidable questions—according to the authors, this device would have materialized a shift from the facilitation of technical troubleshooters to the legitimization of creative troublemakers. In that vein, Fischer and Cretu present what they call a "speculative remake" of the *Ashby Box*. Respecting the "black-boxedness" of Ashby's machine—i.e., without opening it—they use technical knowledge and historical records to develop operative remakes of the cybernetician's device. Consequently, they demonstrate how the *frictions* between what is graspable and unknowable in complex machines also signals the *frictions* between the predictability that makes life survivable and the unpredictability that makes life interesting.

Finally, the book concludes with Hans-Christian von Herrmann's epilogue *"The Cybernetic Revolution."* There, the author first traces the genealogies that from the 1980s onwards positioned cybernetics as a transformative element within the German-speaking humanities. This transformation impacted its scholarly production, the very definition of some of its fields and academic programs, as well as the philosophical foundations of these inquiries. From such a topology, von Herrmann also outlines archaeological ties that seem to connect discussions that took place in the German-speaking world of the early 19th century with the conceptual frameworks that made the emergence of cybernetics as a proper field of research possible over 100 years later. In other words, von Herrmann describes an epistemological drive—first as a latency, then as an actuality—that has played, and continues to play, a key role in the intellectual production of this corner of the world. The attention to the relations between technique, technology, and human beings, and thus between those elements and their context and environment, would then respond to a broad historical and philosophical impetus which would have found in cybernetics the main endeavor for its concretization. Therefore, by emphasizing the enduring presence of these issues in the foundations and history of German media studies, the author not only underlines the relevance of the hypotheses sustaining this volume and thus of the works here presented, but also the role of *cybernetic thinking* in the development of our contemporaneity into a conglomerate of overly complex systems.

Paraphrasing Claus Pias (2004, 9), it is time to come back to cybernetics; time to develop a *broader* understanding by endeavoring to revisit cybernetics' genealogy, re-inquire into its archives, and re-analyze its machines—or perhaps even re-construct them. Beyond the interests the first crises of the Internet may have triggered over 20 years ago, the current reasons for such a return are, if not different, deeper and more complex. The everyday evidence of algorithmization, and its, as it were, tangible reality, makes this enterprise an urgent one. In the face of Big Data analytics (Rouvroy and Berns 2013) and the increasing ubiquity of AI machines (Pasquinelli 2015), the technological platforms and networks entangled with our daily lives seem to be echoing cybernetic systems. To what extent are they not based on upgraded and insurmountably complex operations of feedback? Are they not able to inform themselves, or to be fed by, the environments they encompass? What are the elements,

16 the actors, and the dynamics shaping or rather operating those environments? While this volume does not aim to provide comprehensive answers to these questions, it does outline concrete paths to tackle them. All the more, this book understands itself as a probe; one sent in search of others that can join in this inquiry. After all, in order to maintain the functionality and stability of these frictions, the vastitude of these systems requires a multitude.

Berlin, February 2023.

References

Ernst, Wolfgang. 2018. "Radical Media Archaeology (its epistemology, aesthetics and case studies)." *Artnodes* 21 (2018): 35–43. http://dx.doi.org/10.7238/a.v0i21.3205.

Foucault, Michel. 1972. *The Archaeology of Knowledge: And the Discourse of Language.* New York: Pantheon Books.

Hörl, Erich, and Michael Hagner. 2008. "Überlegungen zur kybernetischen Transformation des Humanen." In *Die Transformation des Humanen: Beiträge zur Kulturgeschichte der Kybernetik*, edited by Michael Hagner and Erich Hörl, 7–37. Frankfurt am Main: Suhrkamp.

Humboldt-Universität. n.d. "Applied Cybernetics Lecture Series." Accessed January 19, 2023. https://hu.berlin/applied_cybernetics.

Kittler, Friedrich. (1989/1993) 1997. "The World of the Symbolic—A World of the Machine." In *Literature, Media, Information Systems*, edited by John Johnston, 130–46. Amsterdam: OPA Amsterdam B.V.

Kline, Ronald R. 2015. *The Cybernetic Moment: Or Why We Call Our Age the Information Age.* Baltimore: Johns Hopkins University Press.

Medina, Eden. 2011. *Cybernetic Revolutionaries: Technology and Politics in Allende's Chile.* Cambridge: MIT Press.

Müggenburg, Jan. 2017. "Bats in the Belfry: On the Relationship of Cybernetics and German Media Theory." *Canadian Journal of Communication* 42 (3): 467–84. https://doi.org/10.22230/cjc.2017v42n3a3214.

Pasquinelli, Matteo. 2015. "Introduction." In *Alleys of Your Mind: Augmented Intelligence and Its Traumas*, edited by Matteo Pasquinelli, 7–18. Lüneburg: meson press.

Pias, Claus. 2004. "Zeit der Kybernetik—Eine Einstimmung." In *Cybernetics | Kybernetik: The Macy-Conferences 1946–1953, Volume 2—Essays and Documents/ Essays und Dokumente*, edited by Claus Pias, 9–41. Zürich: diaphanes.

Pickering, Andrew. 2002. "Cybernetics and the Mangle: Ashby, Beer and Pask." *Social Studies of Science* 32 (3): 413–37.

Rouvroy, Antoinette, and Thomas Berns. 2013. "Gouvernementalité algorithmique et perspectives d'émancipation: Le disparate comme condition d'indiv duation par la relation?" *Réseaux* 177 (1): 163–96. https://doi.org/10.3917/res.177.0163.
Žižek, Slavoj, Frank Ruda, and Agon Hamza. 2022. *Reading Hegel*. Cambridge: Polity.

HELMUT KRAUCH

SYSTEMS RESEARCH

CYBERNETICS

WEST GERMANY

THE RAND CORPORATION

HEIDELBERG STUDY GROUP

From Delphi to ORAKEL: A Brief Media History of Computer Democracy

Eva Schauerte

This chapter discusses the scope and media-historical relevance of the political debate TV show ORAKEL. Produced and broadcast by West Germany's Public Broadcasting Network in association with other TV channels in the early 1970s, it is argued here that this program constitutes a seminal example of a social and political use of cybernetics in Germany. Based on Helmut Krauch's work on systems research at the Heidelberg Study Group, the ORAKEL TV show faced both technological and political frictions. Beyond being mere problems, this chapter contends that these obstacles were an essential component of this case's character and thus of this project's relevance.

ORACLE

On December 30, 1971, *ORAKEL über das Fernsehen*—Oracle on
Television—a social experiment operating live *on* and *with* television, entered its second season. The acronym ORAKEL stood for
"Organized Representative Articulation of Critical Development
Gaps," designating a TV series through which West Germany's
public broadcasting network (WDR)—in cooperation with its
South-West German counterpart (SWF)—tested the direct
participation of viewers in the discussion and decision-making
around questions of "environmental protection" and "television"
from 1971 to 1972. The basic concept of the experiment consisted
of the live discussion of a panel of experts in a TV studio, which
was however interrupted and guided by interventions coming
from the audience. A panel of citizens, selected to represent a
cross-section of society, as well as a group of scientists, could
intervene directly in the discussion. Additionally, viewers at home
had the opportunity to give their opinion on the issues discussed
in the program via telephone, fax, or even letter, thus helping to
shape the decision-making process. This feedback was thus evaluated and explained live by two analysts in the studio. The broadcast was crowded with technical support and students taking
calls and transcribing the answers into punched cards. Moreover, a myriad of technical devices—telephones, fax machines,
flip charts, teleprinters, punched card readers, computers
themselves—but also papers, cables, and multiple plugs lying
around and blocking the way, occupied large portions of the set.

ORAKEL's first season had already been broadcast a few
months earlier. On the topic of "environmental protection,"
representatives from the industry and the state, a poet from the
political left, as well as a professor of medicine from the state
health department discussed the issue. The debate allowed for
productive interjections and was thus steered by the panel, data
sets, and the audience. Accordingly, the mastermind behind this
format, Helmut Krauch, concluded in retrospect:

This organized conflict would certainly not have differed from a normal, more or less boring expert panel discussion. But the direct interventions of the audience and the intervening call phases made it exciting. *Werner Höfer* later said it was as exciting as a soccer World Cup. (Krauch 1972, 64)[1]

Almost 3,000 calls had been received and processed in the course of the broadcast. Nevertheless, viewers who were not able to make it through, attempted to personally reach both the show's director Werner Höfer and WDR's Klaus von Bismarck, even breaking into "the broadcasting room in order to make themselves heard" (Krauch 1972, 66). Krauch points out that technical systems to process the calls more quickly and display them on the screen had long been available, so that the discussion should not be interrupted. But the production of the show had a limited budget, and therefore they had to hope for the viewers' patience. The positive side, however, was

> that about 80 percent of the participants believed that ORAKEL could be used to determine viewers' opinions, and about 95 percent of them wanted to participate again in a new experiment. About two thirds even wanted ratings determined by ORAKEL to be considered in policy decisions. (Krauch 1972, 69)

Although Krauch and his colleagues continued working on the ORAKEL broadcasts, their format was slightly changed. Against Krauch's strong protest, the scientists' data sets were largely dismissed on the grounds that the debate already had enough expertise—i.e., the expert panel—and that an additional element would confuse viewers even more.

Even if the program was initially a complete success in terms of audience response, receiving more than 6,000 calls on "a total of nine questions posed in three call phases" (Krauch 1972, 77), the audience did not show a deep connection with the debated

1   All quotes from sources in German translated by the author.

 issues—with the exception of environmental protection. Krauch therefore suggested that if ORAKEL was to continue, it should focus on topics with a stronger connection to the future, as this was one of the system's strengths. He also wanted to have the technical equipment that would allow the discussion to proceed uninterrupted during a simultaneous call phase, that could thus be evaluated and fed into the discussion. Additionally, it would also be advisable to be able to spontaneously change the participants of the debate if they behaved too passively. All in all, it was desirable to have fewer disturbances that would interrupt the viewing experience and the flow of information.

From the perspective of media studies and cultural history, however, it is precisely the technical malfunctions and deficits—the home-made and improvised aids and props—as well as the awkward structure of the show in relation to today's television, that remain of interest. These aspects display the inherent mediality of television, the noise in the channel: either when the host Hans Aalborn repeatedly dropped a sticking number eight piece, when the questions system showed questions upside down, when the display boards did not work and a piece of paper was instead filmed or something was quickly written down, when the ringing of telephones and the noise of the card punchers invaded all in the studio, or when the analysts—described by one viewer as "bastards from the database"—were once again disappointed to discover that they could not derive any differences from the genders and social backgrounds in the answers—all this, in retrospect, has a comedic character. In the early 1970s, however, ORAKEL's proneness to interference fueled both the debate about a cybernetic self-administration of society—as initiated by Helmut Krauch elsewhere—and the discourse surrounding the possibilities for an informed audience to participate in the new broadcasting media—for which Hans Magnus Enzensberger, among others, stands out with his *construction kit for a theory of the media* (Enzensberger 1970). Krauch himself later stated

that the instrument of "critical publicity" proposed by Jürgen
Habermas was not by itself sufficient as a parapet against

> constructed opinions … According to Enzensberger's
> suggestions, technical possibilities should be used to create
> reversible information structures—i.e., to enable every
> citizen not only to retrieve information from databases—but
> also to influence these media through direct contacts and
> interventions. However, this process would not be completed
> until power over the dissemination of new knowledge and
> the design of new technology was exercised by the entire
> population. For only then would the databases and infor-
> mation storage be filled with knowledge and facts that also
> correspond to the demands and problems of the present.
> (Krauch 1972, 37–38)

As one of the heads of the Heidelberg Study Group for Systems
Research, Helmut Krauch was also an advisor to West Germany's
government during the 1960s and 1970s. Initially subordinate
to the Federal Ministry for Atomic Affairs, the Heidelberger
group was devoted to questions of both *research planning* and
technology assessment on the US approach. In 1962 for example,
the group undertook—in cooperation with the "Rationalization
Board of the German Economy" (*Rationalisierungs-Kuratorium
der Deutschen Wirtschaft*)—a study trip to the USA during which
Krauch and his colleagues visited several scientific institutions—
e.g., The National Science Foundation, the RAND Corporation, the
MITRE Corporation, the Stanford Research Institute, etc. (Krauch,
Kunz, and Rittel 1966, 7–10)—in order to get a picture of the
relation between government-funded scientific research and politics in that country. With Jürgen Habermas as their "intellectual
crowd-puller" (*intellektuelle[n] Zugpferd*) (Brinckmann 2006, 102;
also Habermas 1968), the group developed a pragmatic model
for policy advice that positioned itself against both decisionist
and technocratic models. It envisaged the active involvement of
an informed public in the processes of political decision-making,
and was based on the circular flow and translation of scientific

research and everyday problems in an ongoing communication (Habermas 1968, 134–35). This communicative "interrelation" between politics and science should be genuinely democratic and thus, at the same time, suitable for preventing ideological politics:

> In place of a strict separation between the functions of the expert and the politician, the pragmatic model precisely entails a critical interrelationship that not only strips an ideologically supported exercise of rule of an unreliable basis of legitimacy, but on the whole makes it accessible to scientifically guided discussion and thereby substantially changes it. (Habermas 1968, 126)

It is this idea of futurology and the interlocking of science and politics through communication that Helmut Krauch embraced, and that was further developed by the Heidelberg Study Group in a "planning system approach" (Brinckmann 2006, 102). The core of Krauch's resulting "political cybernetics," or of his "cybernetic social research," was the continuous feedback of information between the environment and the "science-politics interaction system"—as science and technology historian Andrea Brinckmann aptly summarizes, this was intended for its constant "behavioral correction" (Brinckmann 2006, 105; also Schauerte 2019, 178–180). Regulation, feedback, and communication thus became the basis of a system that involved citizens in decision-making.

The ORAKEL broadcasts by WDR can therefore be understood as an experiment in which this form of political cybernetics would be put into practice. The criticism of such experiments was enormous. Even during the first season on environmental protection, politicians Katharina Focke (Social Democratic Party of Germany, SPD) and Hanna-Renate Laurien (Christian Democratic Union of Germany, CDU)[2] criticized the danger and questioned whether

---

2   The SPD politician Katharina Focke was also Federal Minister for Youth, Family, and Health in the governments of chancellors Willy Brandt and Helmut Schmidt from 1972 to 1976. The CDU politician Hanna-Renate

the ORAKEL system added any actual value in the context of parliamentary democracy. Similarly, a number of national and international press reports were also devoted to the debate (Groh 1970; Dippner 1970; Moos 1971; Thielepape 1971; Stehr 1971; Heinemann 1971; Silcock 1971; Rogers 1971). As an Austrian political scientist and television critic—who attended one of the expert panel discussions led by Werner Höfer at the Berlin Radio Exhibition in 1971—summed up:

> I find this particular ORAKEL to be a prime example of smoke and mirrors; as this magical land—or as it is called here, the "TV wonderland"—sees the "EDP (Electronic Data Processing) wonderland" being added to it. The whole thing stands on a giant pedestal. Then some beautiful words such as panel, etc. are added; in this case, not only the "love-in" but now also the "come-in." I mean that, through using EDP in order to be lifted into an even higher sphere of incomprehensibility, an even greater gulf is created. (Krauch 1972, 87)

Delphi

The US role models from the RAND Corporation had a significant influence on Krauch's research, even though he located himself and the study group in a politically and socially different zone—i.e., much further to the left. Nevertheless, Krauch admired the work of his colleagues in the USA, especially their inter-disciplinary, unconventional, independent, and yet politically effective approach to consulting. An instrument for decision-making and futurology, developed by RAND researchers Norman Dalkey, Nicholas Rescher, and Olaf Helmer in the 1950s, con-stituted an important source of inspiration for the development of the ORAKEL system: namely, the Delphi method.

Laurien, also known as "Hanna Granata" because of her temperament, held roles such as Minister of Culture of Rhineland-Palatinate (1976–81) and Mayor of Berlin from 1986 to 1989.

First presented in 1951 in a memorandum on the "Use of Experts for the Estimation of Bombing Requirements" (Dalkey and Helmer 1951), and then condensed into a separate report in 1962, the method developed by RAND optimized decision-making processes through a multi-level expert consensus (Dalkey and Helmer 1962)—in Dalkey's words, "'to cream the tops of the heads' of a group of knowledgeable people." (Dalkey 1969, 16). A crucial feature of the method was the constant repetition of interviews with controlled feedback. The basic experiment from 1951 tasked a handpicked group of experts with identifying, from the perspective of a Soviet strategic planner, the optimal targets for attacking US soil. Similarly, the experiment also asked the experts for the number of atomic bombs needed to destroy those targets, and thus weaken the US defense industry by a given factor. To do this, the seven experts—four economists, one physicist specializing in "physical-vulnerability" (Dalkey and Helmer 1951, 5), one systems analyst, and one electrical engineer—were interviewed in five rounds. During this multi-stage procedure, the participants were provided with a summary of the results and arguments after each round. Additional information was also supplied when necessary, as the experts were confronted with changing destruction factors, follow-up questions, and figures, while avoiding direct contact between them for the entire time (fig. 1). After increasing the most moderate answer from 50 to 167 bombs, and the highest estimate being reduced from 5,000 to 360 bombs, the researchers saw their experiment and the pragmatic power of the Delphi method confirmed for the first time:

> There are strong indications that, if the experiment had been continued through a few more rounds of questionnaires, the median would have shown a downward trend and the ratio of the largest to the smallest answer would have shrunk to 2 or less. (Dalkey and Helmer 1962, 16)

Questions about the selection and composition of the group of experts—e.g., why only one physicist was consulted as opposed

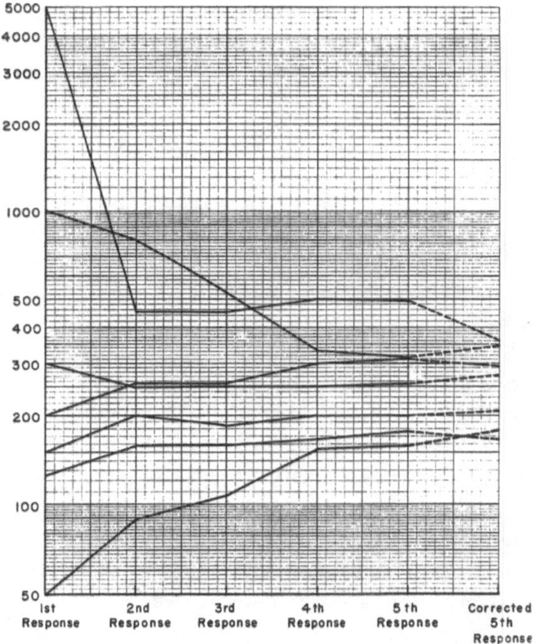

[Fig. 1] Graph on "Successive Estimates" derived from Experts Group Responses (Source: Dalkey and Helmer 1962, 15). Courtesy of the RAND Corporation.

to four economists—remained untouched in the subsequent revisions of the experiment, as did the problem of the result being difficult to verify empirically.[3]

Nevertheless, the experiments continued and the Delphi method became an integral part of future research projects, not only in the framework of the RAND Corporation. Especially due to computerization, Delphi experienced a revival in the 1970s and 1980s, and it is still a common tool in social research today.

3   A more detailed discussion on the epistemological background of the Delphi method in the context of the RAND corporation has been developed elsewhere by the author (Schauerte 2016; 2019, 171–73).

However, while the first Delphi experiments dealt with clearly delineated, easily quantifiable problems, the actual goal of the method quickly became clear. It involved the direct linking of consultation and decision:

> Just as we can use Delphi in the traditional way to explore the prospects of a group consensus regarding "what the facts are (or—in predictive applications—will be)," so we can deploy it on the issue of "what to do." (Rescher 1969, 2)

At the same time that Krauch's experiments were being carried out in West Germany in the early 1970s, work was also being done in the USA to improve and expand the scope of Delphi with the help of new media technologies. Accordingly, the mathematician and physicist Murray Turoff—a specialist in computer-mediated communication—conducted an experiment for the Office of Emergency Preparedness, Executive Office of the US President. As early as 1970, he investigated the use of Delphi as a computer-supported conference system—i.e., a "Delphi on a Delphi" (Turoff 1972, 179, 199; see also Bommer 1972, 15). Some of the advantages of this Delphi conference system—which was also based on the repetition of anonymous questions and on feeding information into the communication circuit—involved above all enormous time savings, both regarding the organization of the system and its use:

> One significant contribution of the computer to the communication process is elimination of the normal round structure of the Delphi with accompanying weeks of delay in feedback to the group. Therefore, one has essentially a real-time communication structure for the group interaction. (Turoff 1972, 183–84)

All the more, according to Turoff, the experiment marked the actual birth of artificial intelligence. Until then, the possibilities of computers had not been adequately exploited, but the connection between the Delphi method and modern computer technologies would be the first step in making the computer a true extension of man's intellectual capability ... In essence, this philosophy of the design for interactive computer systems would be to maximize the ability of humans, who are the primary source of the information, to supply it directly to the computer for accumulation, correlation, analyses, and dissemination. (Turoff 1972, 184)

This computer-based Delphi method also experienced a boom due to growing concerns regarding other analytical or financial modeling techniques, thus becoming a popular tool among futurologists and decision-makers.

Helmut Krauch himself emphasized the benefits of such computerized Delphi procedures. On the one hand, users would remain in their familiar information network and would have easier access to their documents, as well as the possibility of exchanging information with colleagues. Furthermore, the factors of alienation caused by an artificial experimental situation would be eliminated. Participants would not need to be present for the entire time, being able to opt in and out at their own discretion, depending on how important (or not) the discussed issues were for them (Krauch 1972, 105–06). Krauch saw this as an important innovation of the Delphi method, putting it precisely on the path to the computer democracy he aimed for; another "technical model for a complicated program planning and control system," which Krauch cites in a footnote, was "the TOPICS system ... which has been operated successfully for years at the Japanese Broadcasting Corporation ... and is distinguished precisely by its ability to coordinate and harmonize" (Krauch 1972, 152).[4]

4   Furthermore, Project Cybersyn, developed by Stafford Beer in Chile, represents another reference from the early 1970s (Medina 2011).

Computer Democracy

According to Krauch, the computer—linked to other communication media—was primarily intended to simplify communication within and between political stakeholders and working groups—but also between these groups and politics, as well as with consulting science (Krauch 1972, 100–02). The aforementioned ORAKEL thus represents an attempt to put the pragmatic political consulting model of the Heidelberg Study Group into practice, which not only places politics and science in interrelation, but also declares the general public as the central element in the communication circuit it sets.

Krauch elaborated on these considerations in his 1972 book *Computer Democracy*. Moreover, the book is at the same time a plea for a new planning ideology, and a manifesto of *scientific policy advice* based on the productive connection of the knowledge of the population with the *"truth of science."* In this context, planning is no longer understood merely as crisis management. Planning, according to Krauch, "is more than just producing plans" (Krauch 1972, 91).

> Solutions to problems, and decisions, would have to be prepared that are "oriented to tomorrow's state of social development as well as the day after tomorrow, instead of that of yesterday." If one really wants this, one would have to use new methods of futurology, simulation, and experimental decision research. (Krauch 1972, 91)

In this context, Krauch called for a decentralized communication and planning system to actively involve society in political planning (Krauch 1972, 100). Organized in groups devoted to research, handling problems, coordination, project management, and innovation as well as efficiency and information, citizens would get involved and get informed. All groups would be connected to data repositories, which would be continuously updated by the groups themselves as well as by experts.

Transparency in terms of communication with, between, and within the groups was a top priority. In general, communication was the central element of Krauch's theory, because only permanent communication led to the continuous self-correction of the system. Computers should help facilitate this communication, and thus encourage more citizens to participate. An in-person meeting of the groups was intended to only rarely take place, but instead

> participants remain at their workstations or at home and are connected only via a data center and the database—which also has a secretarial function. The communication channels in this case are the telephone or the mail. For experimental purposes, input and output devices equipped with screens are already being connected directly to the computer. In 10, or at the latest 20 years, these communication difficulties will most likely be overcome, because network switching will then be possible via electronic fully automatic dial exchanges and the push-button and videophone, as well as through extensively developed cable television. (Krauch 1972, 105)

The goal of this type of computer democracy was the "extensive self-control of people as individuals and as a social group" (Krauch 1972, 119), but also a multifaceted knowledge acquisition. This is because Krauch's version of cybernetic self-governance should not only lead to making the best decisions for the common good, but also help ensure that one is "no longer only guessing at their goals and needs, but can rather grasp them, express them, pass them on to others, and be able to pursue them together with others." (Krauch 1972, 105). To achieve this, computer democracy had to start at the root of society—i.e., in educational institutions. According to Krauch, even children should be involved in planning which is oriented towards problem-solving and decision-making, through learning existing rules and evidence (Krauch 1972, 120–22). In general, Krauch's statements seem less connected to a techno-utopia than to a social one. In addition to educating citizens so that they may become a mature, committed, critical public, the latter also focuses on the integration of what he called the "lower classes." Not only in the treatment he gave to the topic in the press, but already during the ORAKEL broadcasts, Krauch repeatedly addressed the low participation of socially and economically disadvantaged citizens, arguing that his computer democracy also aimed at the long-term elimination of social inequalities. As early as 1963, he described the Heidelberg Study Group as a large-scale research institute "concerned with the analysis of social situations in relation to what is technically possible, targeting the solving of urgent problems that are of the broadest economic and social interest." (Krauch 1963). However, the publication of his ideas on computer democracy and their pop-cultural treatment by the ORAKEL TV show coincided exactly with the period in which the study group increasingly fell into disfavor due to the change of government in 1969. Andrea Brinckmann concludes:

> In 1971, the ambitious project for a comprehensive system analysis of [West Germany's] Chancellery had virtually failed; a project carried out as part of the no less ambitious plans of Chancellery head [Horst] Ehmke to transform the office into a state-of-the-art government headquarters. When it became totally clear that the research approach deployed by [the Heidelberg] Study Group could not be used to present quick reform and rationalization results to the public, the group no longer found sufficient support amid the increasing fatigue on government policy planning of the 1970s. (Brinckmann 2011, 24)

In the following years, due to a lack of political support—also as a result of criticism from Horst Ehmke, the Chief of Staff at the German Chancellery, who had excessively interfered with content—the Study Group was dissolved and its different areas of work were absorbed by West Germany's other federal institutions of futurology and planning. Thus, the Group's "Information and Documentation" department became part of the Society for Information and Documentation (*Gesellschaft für*

Information und Dokumentation, GID), which had been founded in Frankfurt in the early 1970s, and the "Planning and Decision" department led by Krauch was incorporated into the Karlsruhe Nuclear Research Center run by the nuclear physicist Wolf Häfele. Over several phases, this center evolved into the Institute for Technology Assessment and Systems Analysis (ITAS), which is still active today (Brinckmann 2006). Krauch's disappointment would become visible, Brinckmann argues, in the critical tone of *Computer Democracy*:

> Contrary to Krauch's earlier views, this book about h s ORAKEL experiment was utopian in character, driven in part by the frustrating realization that during the [Heidelberg Study Group's] nearly 15 years of existence, citizen participation in solving planning problems made little progress. (Brinckmann 2011, 34)

Against this background, it is particularly remarkable that West Germany's Broadcasting Network, and the other three cooperating channels, had offered a platform to disseminate the critical, planning, and problem-oriented approach of the study group, bringing it to public attention. The technical shortcomings and improvisatory nature of the program were finally attributed to its avant-garde ideas. The closing remarks of the presenter Hans Ahlborn, delivered well after midnight on New Year's Eve 1971/72, made for a fitting summation: "And keep in mind that with this program we are ahead of the curve for the communication possibilities of this time!"

References

Bommer, Jürgen. 1972. "Computergestützte DELPHI-Konferenz: Konzeption und Bericht über ein Experiment." *Analysen und Prognosen* 19 (1): 15–22.

Brinckmann, Andrea. 2006. *Wissenschaftliche Politikberatung in den 60er Jahren: die Studiengruppe für Systemforschung, 1958 bis 1975*. Berlin: Sigma.

———.2011. "Die Heidelberger 'Studiengruppe für Systemforschung' (SfS): zur Entwicklung von Systemforschung und Politikberatung in der Bundesrepublik Deutschland 1958–1975." In Systemforschung: Politikberatung und öffentliche

34   Aufklärung, edited by Reinhard Coenen and Karl-Heinz Simon, 20–41. Kassel: Kassel University Press.

Dalkey, Norman. 1969. *The Delphi Method: An Experimental Study of Group Opinion.* RAND Report RM-5888-PR. RAND Corporation. https://www.rand.org/pubs/research_memoranda/RM5888.html.

Dalkey, Norman, and Olaf Helmer. 1951. *The Use of Experts for the Estimation of Bombing Requirements.* RAND Report R-1283-PR. RAND Corporation.

———.1962. *An Experimental Application of the Delphi Method to the Use of Experts.* RAND Report RM-727/1. RAND Corporation. https://www.rand.org/pubs/research_memoranda/RM727z1.html.

Dippner, Helmut. 1970. "Zukunftswünsche werden durch 'ORAKEL' ermittelt." *Frankfurter Rundschau*, October 7, 1970.

Enzensberger, Hans Magnus. 1970. "Baukasten zu einer Theorie der Medien." *Kursbuch* 20 (March): 159–86.

Erd, Rainer. 1972. "Forschungsförderung im Fernsehsessel?" *Frankfurter Rundschau*, 1972.

———.1972. "'Fernseher' rufen nach Mitbestimmung." *Hersfelder Zeitung*, January 3, 1972.

Groh, D. 1970. "Bestimmt der Bürger die Planung?" *Publik* 48 (1970): 37.

Habermas, Jürgen. 1968. "Verwissenschaftlichte Politik und öffentliche Meinung." In *Technik und Wissenschaft als "Ideologie,"* edited by Jürgen Habermas, 120–45. Frankfurt am Main: Suhrkamp.

Heinemann, F. J. 1971. "Der Zuschauer hat das Wort." *Stuttgarter Zeitung*, December 30, 1972.

Krauch, Helmut. 1963. "Die Wissenschaft in der Wirtschaft." *Handelsblatt*, December 28, 1963.

———.1972. *Computer-Demokratie.* Düsseldorf: VDI-Verlag.

Krauch, Helmut, Werner Kunz, and Horst Rittel, eds. 1966. *Forschungsplanung: Eine Studie über Ziele und Strukturen amerikanischer Forschungsinstitute.* Munich: R. Oldenbourg.

Medina, Eden. 2011. *Cybernetic Revolutionaries: Technology and Politics in Allende's Chile.* Cambridge: MIT Press.

Moos, M. 1971. "Der Zuschauer wird mobilisiert." *Süddeutsche Zeitung*, 1971.

Rescher, Nicholas. 1969. *Delphi and Values.* RAND Report P-4182. RAND Corporation. http://www.rand.org/pubs/papers/P4182.html.

Rogers, Peter. 1971. "Box Populi." *The Guardian*, May 7, 1971.

Schauerte, Eva. 2016. "Von Delphi zu Hyperdelphi—mediale Praktiken des Beratens und die Entscheidung des Unentscheidbaren." In *Medien der Entscheidung*, edited by Tobias Conradi, Florian Hoof, and Rolf Nohr, 67–86. Münster: LIT.

———.2019. *Lebensführungen: Eine Medien- und Kulturgeschichte der Beratung.* Paderborn: Wilhelm Fink.

Silcock, Bryan. 1971. "You Too Can Govern the Nation's Future." *The Sunday Times*, July 18, 1971.

Stehr, J. 1970. "System ORAKEL." *Der Spiegel*, October 25, 1970. https://www.spiegel.de/politik/system-orakel-a-6fef605b-0002-0001-0000-000043787163.

———.1971. "Jetzt können die Zuschauer beim Fernsehen mitreden." *TV Hören und Sehen*.

Thielepape, M. 1971. "Wozu ein 'organisierter Konflikt' dient." *Rhein-Neckar-Zeitung*, 1971.

Turoff, Murray. 1972. "Delphi Conferencing: Computer-Based Conferencing with Anonymity." *Technological Forecasting and Social Change* 3 (1): 159–204. https://doi.org/10.1016/S0040-1625(71)80012-4.

SYSTEMS ANALYSIS

COLD WAR

AUSTRIA

WORLD DYNAMICS

MODELS

ENVIRONMENT

[2]

From Cybernetics to Sustainability: Negotiating the World Problematic at IIASA (1972–1989)

Isabell Schrickel

This chapter focuses on the establishment and the research developments of the International Institute for Applied Systems Analysis (IIASA) in Austria, as a key case study to understand the historical and epistemological connections between cybernetics and sustainability thinking. It is argued that by paying attention to the politics and the shared concerns that informed the foundation of IIASA, as well as to the research frameworks and policy pro- posal developed by the Institute from the early 1970s onwards, it becomes clear that essential elements of cybernetic thinking remain part and parcel of the emerging field of sustain- ability science. It is also contended here that

even if the Institute was in itself a product of the Cold War, it operated paradigmatically as a platform to move the world problematic from the fragmented and antagonistic logic of that period, to a global, interconnected understanding of the common *real*.

While the waves of excitement around cybernetics had abated in the West by the 1960s, the discipline gained more traction among the scientists and modernizers of the political system in the Soviet Union. Foreign policy circles within President Lyndon B. Johnson's administration took advantage of this interest and sought to position the field as a potential area of international scientific cooperation. They proposed to use it as a pathway both for the introduction of Western ideas of management to the East, as well as for accessing their mathematical expertise. At the time, one of the central ideas discussed among Johnson's advisors was the initiative to establish an "East-West Institute of Management and Administration" (Bator 1966). Although the immediate purpose and mission of such an institute remained relatively vague at the beginning, it was "based on the proposition that all advanced economies—capitalist, socialist, communist—share the problem of efficiently managing large programs and enterprises: factories and cities, subway systems and air traffic, hospitals and water pollution" (Bator 1966, 1). Over many years of negotiations the joint research center on the "problems of modern societies" (IIASA Charter 1972) became a reality, and in 1972 the International Institute for Applied Systems Analysis (IIASA) opened its doors in the Austrian town of Laxenburg, near Vienna.

Research projects at IIASA were conducted by multidisciplinary teams of social and natural scientists, systems analysts, mathematicians, and policy experts from both sides of the Iron Curtain. While the negotiations were taking place, a wide range of environmental problems entered the public debate worldwide.

In the light of these concerns, IIASA would focus much of its work on the society-environment nexus, and on the complex problems that similarly occurred in all advanced societies, such as transboundary environmental pollution, or issues such as sustainable energy supply, the resilience of ecosystems, and infrastructure planning. More substantially, however, the work developed at the Institute also focused on the study of newly emerging global issues like climate change and world population growth. Years later, international policymakers and experts began to discuss these issues as problems of sustainable development, building an expertise that was often based on the early work conducted at IIASA.

Accordingly, this chapter discusses IIASA as a pivotal institution where, after the 1970s, cybernetic thinking was further developed in an international context and applied to new problem areas, but also received criticism and disenchantment in the light of new global challenges. Several projects at IIASA reveal the persistence of the powerful imaginary standpoint of cybernetics, which seemed to believe that there was an engineering solution to all kinds of problems modern societies faced. However, the intellectual debates at IIASA also show the emergence of an understanding about the limitations of control and hard systems approaches; an understanding that positioned cybernetics in the context of the development of post-positivist epistemologies and innovative fields of sustainability science.

In this sense, a discussion of the research developed at IIASA, and an assessment of its historical role, may at first seem in conflict with the predominant accounts of cybernetics. Most histories of cybernetics in the United States tell a story of success: how the new science of machines emerged together with the theory of information shortly after World War II, and how it reached a peak with the adoption and modification of its concepts by other disciplines in the 1950s and 1960s—but also, of course, how this peak ended when cybernetics lost its status as a universal science around 1970. In other parts of the world, however, cybernetics took quite different paths, ranging from an emphasis on the performative character of cybernetic machines in Britain, to a more philosophical style of cybernetics prevailing in France and Germany, or its late manifestation as a state science in the Soviet Union (Kline 2015). While these different legacies are well researched by historians, few attempts have been made to understand the historical transformations of cybernetics after the 1970s. Even if the term "cybernetics" quite quickly disappeared from then on, the epistemological regime of cybernetics—in which systems combine both human and nonhuman agents in mutual communication and command—became broader, reaching a level of operativity of historically unprecedented scale.

Driven by such a premise, this chapter points to IIASA as a fundamental case study of this transformation, thus aiming to explore how the contemporary idea of sustainability and some important branches of sustainability science[1] are connected to cybernetics—both historically and epistemologically. This becomes apparent through the particular institutional structure and research designs IIASA deployed in order to study, in an integrated manner, the troublesome trajectories of social, economic, and environmental development. Moreover, this also becomes clear once we acknowledge that sustainability thinking seeks to address multiple interconnected dimensions of human wellbeing that make development sustainable, thus echoing aspects of cybernetics—especially those of the second-order category. Moreover, as we recognize that sustainability science aims to understand unsustainable trajectories of the past to diagnose the causes of problematic developments, and to prescribe interventions to promote transitions, it also becomes evident that its agency makes the episteme of modernity collide against the elusive contemporaneity of modeling frameworks,

---

1   For a detailed discussion on the history of both the notion of sustainability and sustainability science, see Moll 1991; Warde 2018; Caradonna 2018; Clark and Harley 2020.

datasets, and transdisciplinary methods—and then the aforementioned resonances seem to become stronger. As an institutional instantiation of cybernetization, IIASA thus shows that these connections do not, however, obey fluid and positive concatenations, but rather frictional exchanges and adaptations. All interlinked by models, these frictions can be discerned in how both the old and the rising fields tackled questions of long-term developments, cycles, future trajectories, and systems linkages at the Institute. In a word, frictions between the historical, the epistemological, and the political.

A Cybernetic Invitation

In 1967, RAND Corporation analyst Roger E. Levien was tasked with assessing President Lyndon B. Johnson's idea for an international research center devoted to the systematic analysis of the complex problems which advanced and industrialized societies had in common. More importantly, this initiative would be established as a joint effort between the USA and the Soviet Union. In the middle of the Cold War, this sort of scientific cooperation was deployed as a strategic component of the politics of bridge-building towards the East; that is, a politics designed to smooth over international tensions. It was in that context, Levien claimed in his memorandum, that "what the Soviets call 'cybernetics'" made for "an almost ideal candidate for the subject of the institute" (Levien 1967, 1). While being a "vaguely disreputable term" in the West, "thought of as a discipline that makes up in breadth for what it lacks in depth," in the Soviet Union it was perceived as a "positive term" that "gained prestige" through the achievements of its technology and its application to "a wide range of physical, biological, economic, social, and even political problems" (Levien 1967, 1). Dismissed as a misanthropic and bourgeois pseudoscience until Stalin's death, cybernetics indeed gained traction among scientists and modernizers of the political system in the Soviet Union: during the early 1950s, the first mainframe computers—the BESM and the STRELA—were

42 produced in the USSR (Gerovitch 2002, 131–34); in 1954, a review seminar on Western cybernetics was organized at Moscow University (174); in 1957, Sputnik was launched with the assistance of the computers built by local cyberneticians, and in 1958 Norbert Wiener's *Cybernetics* was published in Russian (145–46). Similarly, prominent cyberneticians paid visits to the Soviet Union during the 1960s—Norbert Wiener was in Moscow in 1960, Oscar Morgenstern in 1963, and Ross Ashby in 1964—just as operations research, cybernetics, and management science became well-entrenched in the Soviet academic system (Gerovitch 2002, 58; Rindzevičiūtė 2016, 84–86).

Consequently, Levien recommended taking advantage of the emerging interest in cybernetics in the East, and building upon "the role it has played as a modernizing influence," noticing at the same time the "protection" that the prestige of the term had lent to "a group of nonideological, westward-looking Soviet scientists" (Levien 1967, 1–2). Thus, the deep political-epistemological strategy behind this move also became apparent: cybernetics would not only provide a "pathway for the introduction of Western ideas," (Levien 1967, 1), but also "a science with ideological implications that contradict and challenge the basic tenets of Soviet Marxism-Leninism" (Levien and Maron 1964, 16). Put differently, the RAND analysts were well aware of, as it were, the "poisons" cybernetics "releases in economics, philosophy, psychology, and sociology" (17). For researchers like Levien, cybernetics was both a technology for progress and an "impetus for ideological and political revolution" because it not only provided solutions, but "also presents problems" (24–27).

Media scholars and historians of science have emphasized the different legacies of cybernetics in the East and West (Gerovitch 2002; Kline 2015), but the notion that cybernetics had played a pivotal role in the détente phase of the Cold War by bracketing one of its central projects—i.e., the establishment of IIASA—has so far not really attracted much scholarly attention. Attempting to compensate for that, this chapter argues that the cybernetic invitation to jointly discuss and research key problematic issues affecting the development of modern societies on both sides of the Iron Curtain, as well as tackling emerging global questions, marked both a transformation of cybernetics and the beginning of an epistemic community that shaped new roles for science and scientists. Put differently, the cybernetic approaches deployed at IIASA were conceived as a post-positivist epistemological framework which would in turn be applied to intervene in the future development of modern societies, as well as to explore the future of the global environment and the role of humankind in it (Rindzevičiūtė 2016; Andersson 2018).

The Establishment of IIASA, 1966–1972

In the first week of October in 1972, the high-ranking representatives from 12 national scientific organizations—mostly academies of sciences—gathered at the Royal Society in London to sign an agreement over the establishment of an institution that would mark an unexpected joint venture between the Cold War adversaries. A "non-governmental, multi-national, autonomous scientific institution" was to be established (IIASA Charter 1972, 2). Located at the seam of the Iron Curtain, in Vienna's hinterland, it would be financed in equal parts by the United States, the Soviet Union, and 10 other nations from the East and West, including both German states. With a US citizen as the director and a Russian as the chairman of the council of the institute, it would be named the International Institute for Applied Systems Analysis (IIASA).

The meeting at the Royal Society was convened by Lord Solly Zuckerman. A former chief scientific adviser to the British Government, Zuckerman was also a pioneer in the study of primate behavior and operational research, and one of the founders of the School of Environmental Science at the University of East Anglia. Given that Zuckerman also served as the secretary of the London Zoological Society, the festive dinner the organizers put together for the international guests happened to be held at the Zoo restaurant. There, scientists, academics, and ministry officials from the two, still mutually-antagonistic hemispheres, enjoyed a five-course menu with a selection of French wines from the late 1960s, pleasantly situated right next to the London Zoo orangutans. Among the guests were the president of the United States National Academy of Sciences, the biochemist and nutritionist Philip Handler; the Academy's foreign secretary Harrison Brown, an eco-futurist and professor of geochemistry at the California Institute of Technology; Howard Raiffa and Joseph Bower from Harvard Business School; the vice chairman of the Soviet Union's State Committee for Science and Technology (GKNT) Dzhermen Gvishiani; the deputy director of the Institute of Automation and Remote Control and key expert in control theory and cybernetics in the Soviet Union, who had also initiated the International Federation of Automatic Control (IFAC), Aleksander Letov; the president of the British Royal Society, the Nobel-prize-winning physiologist Alan Hodgkin; the Canadian physicist, science advisor, and founding member of the Club of Rome, J. Rennie Whitehead; the Japanese economist Ken'ichi Miyazawa; the Czechoslovakian economist Tibor Vasko; the vice president of the Polish Academy of Sciences, ballistics and explosives expert Dionizy Smoleński; the leading psychologist and pioneer of artificial intelligence research in East Germany Friedhart Klix; the director of the GDR's Central Committee for Socialist Economic Management Helmut Koziolek; the French physicist and science advisor Maurice Lévy; the secretary general of the Max Planck Society Friedrich Schneider; and the German nuclear physicist Wolf Häfele (Warren 1972; IIASA 1972, 12). The president of the Ford Foundation McGeorge Bundy, the founder of the Club of Rome Aurelio Peccei, and the first president of the *Fondation de France* Pierre Massé sent apologies for being absent. Thus, an unexpected, surprisingly interdisciplinary, and illustrious mixture of scholars celebrated the establishment of IIASA and signed the charter of the Institute, which had been carefully crafted between the chief negotiators from the United

States, the Soviet Union, and the United Kingdom—mainly the former US national security advisor and then-president of the Ford Foundation McGeorge Bundy, the vice chairman of the Soviet Union's State Committee for Science and Technology (GKNT) Dzhermen Gvishiani, and Zuckerman himself. Research topics and approaches, the Institute's name and its location, its purpose, budget, and organizational structure, what pro-portions the Eastern and Western nations should be represented in, as well as the technical equipment for the Institute had been negotiated over years, both in secretive talks among political representatives, and in discussions and conferences among scholars and members of interested organizations in several countries (Riska-Campbell 2011).

Only a month before the ceremony, Vienna prevailed over Fontainebleau, France, as the location for the Institute, as politically-neutral Austria had made the most generous offer: a Habsburg castle in Laxenburg symbolically rented for only one Austrian Schilling per year, the full restoration and maintenance of the building—which had been abandoned in poor condition by the Soviet Army in 1955—and an income-tax-free status for the Institute, as well as several other amendments such as visa facilitation for East German scientists (Zuckerman 1972). Early on, the Austrian ambassador to the Soviet Union Walter Wodak, who had become acquainted with the negotiations about the establishment of the Institute, informed the head of the Austrian government, the socialist chancellor Bruno Kreisky. Because he himself was a strong advocate of European détente, Kreisky became a long-term supporter of IIASA. Accordingly, when the Institute was affected by an unfavorable political climate in the mid-1980s, and the UK and the US withdrew the project, the IIASA Council, in recognition of Kreisky's continuous support, established the "Dr. Bruno Kreisky Lecture Series" for dis-tinguished guests, with Kreisky himself being the first lecturer of the series (Kreisky [1984] 1985).

Finally, the negotiators agreed to formalize in the Institute's charter that IIASA would "initiate and support collaborative and individual research in relation to problems of modern societies arising from scientific and technological development" and that, to this end, it would conduct collaborative research in the "fields of systems analysis, cybernetics, operations research, and management techniques" (IIASA 1972, 2).

From Cybernetics to World Modeling

The London gathering, covered in newspapers worldwide, revealed to a broad international audience the scientists' commitment to forge new relations and areas of international collaboration, as they represented some of the most prestigious scientific institutions in the leading industrialized nations. An "East-West Think Tank" was to be established "to seek solutions to problems created by the increasing industrialization of societies," as the *New York Times* reported the day after the dinner (Lyons 1972). Thus, IIASA was among the few tangible, non-military flagship projects of the détente period. With an unprecedented level of direct and professional collaboration, scientists, economists, mathematicians, engineers, policy experts, and systems theoreticians from the East and West further developed fields that had both legendary and contested origins in the military realms of World War II and the Cold War. This collaboration would cover issues that, until then, had been considered to rather be national matters, which did not require international collaboration—particularly not between the Cold War adversaries. These "common problems of modern societies," frequently discussed among the negotiators at the time, were the internationally interdependent projection of energy sources, the management of large-scale industries and information systems, urban and regional planning, transportation, the changes in the physical and biological environment, environmental pollution, and the theory and methodology of systems analysis more generally, as well as its applications to decision making, organization design, and future planning (Raiffa 1972).

In that very sense, the UK's Minister of Trade Michael Noble, who gave the dinner speech at the Zoological Society, stated:

> In the ever-increasing complexity of modern society it is hardly any longer possible for any one person, or even team of people, to evaluate and comprehend problems confronting us and form a rational solution to them. The model of our Society carried by each and every one of us—some say the prejudices we hold—must now be replaced by the objective compilation of data and its processing that goes to make up systems analysis. The age of the computer model is now with us, and, from the heated debates about such models, as applied recently to our environment, it is evident that the Institute is being born at an auspicious moment. (Noble 1972)

Noble clearly referred to the widely influential report *Limits to Growth*, published only a few months before by the Club of Rome (Meadows et al. 1972). The study received a great deal of attention internationally for two principle reasons: first, it connected two strands of discussion of the time—environmentalism and futures studies—at a global scale (Moll 1991); and second, it was based on the methodological innovation of computer simulations which gave the publication a particular scientific appearance. The model had been developed by Jay Forrester, who, with his early work on automatic control and servomechanisms at MIT during the World War II era, could be considered one of the founders of the field of cybernetics. Through his commitment to the Club of Rome, he also became, in a way, a pioneer of sustainability science. In 1956, Forrester moved across campus to the Sloan School of Management where he began applying ideas from cybernetics and control engineering to problems of business and urban planning (Lane and Sterman 2011). After attending a meeting of the Club of Rome in 1970, he developed a "system dynamics" model of the world economy that simulated the interactions between environmental and human systems on a global scale, based on five variables: population, food production, industrialization, pollution, and consumption of nonrenewable natural resources (Forrester 1971). This model was later adapted for the *Limits to Growth* study and different scenarios and predictions were generated—all of which led to rather catastrophic outcomes. The fact that the study had been fundamentally criticized both in terms of its messaging, i.e., its doomsaying, and methodology, i.e., its insufficient database, did not change the fact that it opened up the future of global environmental concern, as well as the role of humankind in the political debate on this matter (Warde, Robin, and Sörlin 2018; Vieille Blanchard 2010). The great public success of *Limits to Growth* inspired several other groups to build similar world models, bringing their alternative perspectives into this emerging sustainability debate. Consequently, in the following years IIASA became an important node in this emerging transnational network of systems thinkers, modelers, and governance experts, where global modeling projects—the "haute couture of world thought" at the time (Nordhaus 1975, 1)—were thoroughly discussed and critically assessed in workshop series and working papers.[2] After a decade of world modeling, these activities were reflected in an experimental volume with the somewhat self-deprecating title *Groping in the Dark*, which the editors understood as a "sociology of a new science struggling with problems too large for the participants but too important to ignore" (Meadows, Richardson, and Bruckmann 1982, back cover)—a clear indication that the focus on a new class of problems was quite a decentering experience for the scientists involved (Leistert and Schrickel 2020).

What role did cybernetics play in these activities? Just as the term "cybernetics" had almost completely disappeared from

---

2 For a general view on this, see in particular IIASA's General Research Area (GEN) in its online repository: https://pure.iiasa.ac.at/view/divisions/prog=5Fgen/.

public debates by the 1970s, it had similarly not left significant
traces in the IIASA corpus. Instead, the methodological work at
the Institute was focused on further developments of systems
analysis, which, understood as an even broader interdisciplinary
approach, built upon earlier work on general systems theory—
where cybernetics was nonetheless an essential element (von
Bertalanffy 1951; 1968; Boulding 1956). For this reason, the
models developed at IIASA were not so much discussed in the
language of cybernetics, as more specialized models and forecasting technologies were developed for particular, less abstract
sets of problems. However, the fascination with world dynamics
and other approaches clearly drew from the idea that complex social systems could be understood and engineered like
technical systems and be subjected to regulation and control.
The cybernetic imagery of flowcharts, adjustable variables, and
feedback mechanisms, remained present in a myriad of variations in the publications produced at IIASA, but the original
engineering context was expanded by incorporating the perspectives and interventions of the observer. Consequently, in
order to explore potential future trajectories and policy options,
IIASA's interdisciplinary projects formulated the problems of
modern societies as sets of complex and dynamic systems,
drawing relations between different geological, biological, social,
and technological spheres. Egle Rindzevičiūtė has argued that
the research conducted at IIASA employed system-cybernetic
ideas to rethink managerial and political practice in order to
understand the role of governance and control when dealing with
complex problems (2016, 8). She has claimed that IIASA therefore
championed a post-positivist epistemology (Rindzevičiūtė 2016,
81; 125) that could also be linked to the *enactive*, constructivist
epistemologies of the observer conceptualized by Heinz von
Foerster in his second-order cybernetics, in which the researcher
faces the challenge and obligation to enter the domain of his own
descriptions (von Foerster [1991] 2003; Scott 2004). With a primal
focus on the actual process of formulating problems—bridging
different disciplines, involving various stakeholders, and iterating

 the problematic—research projects at IIASA sought to enter precisely this domain.

The Making of Sustainability Science at IIASA

Historians of science have studied how, from the 1950s onwards, the notion of *the environment* became a singular global object of a particular kind of future-oriented, managerial, and scientific expertise (Warde, Robin, and Sörlin 2018; Benson 2020). Since then, the environment became relevant in numerous ways, ranging from the national security concerns triggered in the geopolitical context of the early Cold War, to the more recent issues of disquiet stressed by environmental movements, to the contemporary debates around planetary limits. The consolidation of the environment as an epistemological object made it possible for humans and societies to refer to it in various ways—from relations of scarcity (Moll 1991) or catastrophe (Hamblin 2017) to more technical and engineering types of environmentalism (Sprenger 2019). The discourse of sustainability—which ultimately linked the environment with development, and, furthermore, with sustainable development—emerged as a particular kind of operational environmentalism, programmatically connected to UN institutions and thus to the growing and reflexive field of sustainability science.

In the last decades, the concepts of sustainable development and sustainability more broadly have acquired a cultural and social dimension that vastly transcends the boundaries of traditional scientific fields. Contemporary definitions describe sustainability science as a field that "differs to a considerable degree in structure, methods, and content from science as we know it" (Kates et al. 2001) and that—with its ambitious agenda of "integrating theory, applied science and policy" (Bettencourt and Kaur 2011, 19540)—addresses the "reconciliation of society's development goals with the planet's environmental limits" (Clark and Dickson 2003, 8059) in "co-productive" ways (Clark and

Harley 2020). Today, there are multiple sustainability science institutions and degree programs at universities worldwide, but it remains unclear where the history of sustainability science as a proper field begins. It is generally assumed that the field had its formal beginnings in the 1980s with important policy documents being published by international institutions, which called for the implementation of new international strategies, as well as for the development of scientific approaches that could respond both to the challenges and opportunities of sustainable development (IUCN, UNEP, and WWF 1980; Brandt 1980; WCED 1987). The most influential of these documents was certainly the report *Our Common Future* authored by the high-profile Brundtland Commission, mandated by the United Nations in 1983. With the most widely quoted definition of sustainable development—that which "meets the needs of the present without compromising the ability of future generations to meet their own needs" (WCED 1987, 43)—the report also launched the compromise formula of "liberal environmentalism" (Bernstein 2001). As a compromise between environmental conservation, economic growth, and social equity, this formula made evident that the pressing environmental concerns of the 1960s and 1970s had ultimately been converted into problems of development by the late 1980s.

In the context of such an agenda, IIASA provided a close institutional fit and was among the few international research institutions consulted by the commission. In effect, the report cited several publications submitted by IIASA researchers, and it is therefore not surprising that some of them later became key players in the emerging field of sustainability science. Thus, while today the field draws from various epistemological cultures, bodies of knowledge, and practices, this chapter argues that some of the most powerful and prevailing frameworks for the understanding and modeling of sustainability problems were developed at IIASA—inscribing in turn the premises and methods of industrialized societies into the field. The Institute thus represents a particular version of sustainability thinking: one that is concerned with the problem of whether—and if so, how—the modern pathway to development could in effect be made sustainable.

In that sense, it is important to consider that, due to its historical legacy as a Cold War institution and so that ideological debates be avoided, normative, political, and ethical questions were, from the outset, excluded from the research initiatives at IIASA. Instead, the problems of modern societies took shape in the interaction of their key technical components—i.e., energy, industry, environment, infrastructure, food, population, and decision systems. Accordingly, two classes of problems were distinguished and studied at the Institute: universal problems—i.e., specific issues common to many nations—and global problems—i.e., concerns relevant to the entire world (Levien 1979).[3]

While many projects at IIASA were in favor of comparative and case studies, others embraced quite inventive experimental approaches to investigate the universal problems affecting modern societies. An example of this can be found in the comparative study on the connections between energy systems and the environment, where regional cases in East Germany, the Rhône-Alpes region of France, and the US state of Wisconsin were analyzed. Existing patterns of energy use and supply, their environmental impacts, as well as their relation to socio-economic patterns, were compared in these different regions in order to advance international discussions on the management of energy resources, examine alternative policies, and develop new forms of communication between modelers and policymakers (Foell 1979).

That latter point—the establishment of innovative communication tools and feedback mechanisms between models and users—was of particular importance for the success of the Institute. It was precisely through this performative dimension

3   Roger E. Levien became IIASA's second director in 1975.

that IIASA tried to make an impact in the real world. In this regard,
C. S. Holling's work on the adaptive assessment and management
of local ecosystems—which earned him a wide professional
reputation beyond the environmental sciences alone—deserves
to be mentioned here as well. The adaptive management process
consists of a carefully designed series of alternating workshops
and research periods in which scientists from different disciplines, policymakers, and other stakeholders come together.
Systems analysts help to identify the different aspects of a
problem, translate them into variables, and integrate them into
a model with which the participants play in order to explore the
potential impacts of different policy options, the responsiveness
of the system under observation, and the responsiveness of the
simulation model itself. The models which were used to foster
such learning experiences were understood as evolving devices
of self-instruction. Holling's approach was tested in numerous
case studies addressing complexities that systems analysts
tended then to ignore—i.e., multiple conflicting decision-makers
and objectives, inter-temporal and intergenerational trade-offs,
and the design of strategies that could deal with the irreducible
uncertainty of the real world (Holling 1978). One of these studies
was conducted in cooperation with the Alpine Research Center
of Innsbruck University, the UNESCO Man and the Biosphere Program (MAB), and the inhabitants of Obergurgl; a Tyrolean Alpine
village that the researchers presented as a microcosm for the
problem of economic growth in relation to limited ecological and
social resources (Holling 1978, 215–42).

More generally, the case study method can be understood as
one of IIASA's key technical gears, since it set in motion a sort of
transmission belt for the circulation of the Institute's expertise,
codes, and conceptualizations. Compared to formal methods
and their rigorous deductive logic and statistical approaches,
the epistemological quality of the case study method involves
instead examining relevant variables in individual cases, making
inferences on which systemic mechanisms may have been

54 at work, or developing historical explanations of particular cases. Consequently, this method and its possibilities became particularly relevant for the Institute, as many of the variables which researchers at IIASA were interested in, such as political culture, are notoriously difficult to operationalize and measure. Case studies allowed them to carry out contextualized comparisons that deliberately sought to address questions of correspondence by searching for analytically equivalent phenomena. Thus, the epistemological features of the case studies approach enabled IIASA researchers to study highly diverse local situations, as well as different policy cultures, connecting them to notions of sustainability in a depoliticized, abstract, and systemic manner. All the more, this method allowed the Institute to compare regions and contexts that, before its establishment, were believed to not have much in common, developing parameters that could from then on be observed and assessed.

An interesting mixture between universal and global approaches can be found in IIASA's Food and Agriculture Program. Aiming to understand national and international policy options in the context of a world of interdependent sovereign nations, the program sought to collaborate in alleviating food problems of the time, as well as preventing the emergence of future ones. Thus, data from all sorts of countries were necessary for this endeavor: whether they had a surplus or a deficit on this matter; if they were exporting or importing nations; and regardless of whether they belonged to the group of developed or developing countries. Consequently, the group developed a piece of software and a set of algorithms connecting the closed national models through a system of international trade linkages, thus being able to evaluate national and international dimensions together, and search for national and international equilibria. Combined with a game-theory method for the testing of policy options, the results of this mixed, national-global approach were published in 1981 in the volume *Food for All in a Sustainable World* (Parikh and Rabár 1981).

Another prominent example to understand the Institute's approach to global issues was the energy program, which was one of IIASA's flagship projects (Schrickel 2017). From its inception and for several years, the program—led by the German physicist and nuclear engineer Wolf Häfele—worked on a global and long-term study of the future of energy systems. The study was based on a model consisting of a set of interconnected sub-systems – similarly to Forrester's *World Dynamics*—and fed with data gathered by dozens of international researchers who were working on the program. The model would provide quantitative evidence for the development of long-term and global scenarios for societal energy supply and demand. In 1981, the results were published in the volume *Energy in a Finite World*, which was prob-ably the first publication to carry the notion of a "sustainable future" in its subtitle (Häfele et al. 1981)—being in turn one of the IIASA works cited in the Brundtland Report. In line with the assumptions of Häfele—who was a strong advocate of nuclear energy—the model showed that a highly energy-demanding planet seemed to be the most likely scenario for the near future.

Nonetheless, IIASA also deserves the attention of historians of sustainability science because it helps reveal controversies engendered in the very problematization of sustainability issues—especially when humanities scholars or critical social scientists were involved. In the case of the energy program, the sociologist Brian Wynne performed the role of the observer, thus entering the domain set out by the project leaders' assumptions. This would lead to the publication of a devastating critique of the energy study in 1984:

> The ... underlying cosmology can be summed up by noting from its own documentation that the conclusions rest upon a simple circularity: The cardinal *assumptions* of the study are a doubling of the world population and a doubling of average per capita income by 2030. But this, along with other lesser assumptions, generates the 'inevitable' conclusion that a sustainable energy future can only be reached by

an expansion of all energy sources as rapidly as physically possible to achieve a minimum rate of economic growth and capital accumulation needed to invest in the capital-intensive technologies (nuclear, synfuels and hard solar) needed for 'sustainability'. In order to achieve this, the initial hypothetical *assumption*, that the doubled population will be so much richer, is converted into a scientifically 'discovered' *requirement*, that the population *must* become this much richer, to supply the needed capital for the 'revealed' capital-intensive, centralized energy technologies! (Wynne 1984, 308)

Even if the research projects discussed in this section had the aim of tackling sustainability questions by deploying a variety of novel and complex systems approaches, the epistemological regime of cybernetic thinking constituted a latent component at IIASA. After all, sustainability problems were formulated as instabilities between the development paths of modern societies and the carrying capacities of their environments; instabilities that could be mediated through policies, technological solutions, or economic instruments in order to reach a desired equilibrium of the overall system. The emergence of a particular version of sustainability science and thinking in the 1980s—both as a field of research and a matter of dispute—therefore seems closely related to the historical legacy of IIASA and the epistemological developments at the Institute.

Conclusion

Through the case of IIASA, this chapter has traced the historical trajectory connecting cybernetics with sustainability science. Conceived during the frosty relations of the Cold War era in the 1960s as an institute for the scientific collaboration between advanced societies on both sides of the Iron Curtain, its founders shared a deep concern about the future development of modern industrialized societies in the changing environment of interdependent economies, and in a context of

shifting values. It has been argued that the research conducted at 57
IIASA during the 1970s and 1980s contributed epistemic frameworks to the emerging idea of sustainable development. As an environmental discourse, this contribution sought to balance the interests of modern societies in particular—i.e., economic growth and environmental protection. It has also been shown that cybernetics not only played a role in the political context in which IIASA was created, but, more substantially, in the epistemic drift the Institute brought about. The fundamental dual character of IIASA—a political bridge apparatus in the context of the Cold War détente phase and a platform of scientific co-production on the complex issues industrial societies were being affected by—speaks of the inherent productivity of *frictions*. All the more, the Institute became a central hub where cybernetic and systems approaches were further developed and combined with new technologies for data analysis, scientific computation, user interaction, and communication. Research projects at IIASA thus re-instantiated and broadened cybernetic methods, transforming them into innovative and increasingly performative and post-positivist fields such as sustainability science.

References

Andersson, Jenny. 2018. *The Future of the World: Futurology, Futurists, and the Struggle for the Post Cold War Imagination*. Oxford: Oxford University Press.

Bator, Francis M. 1966. "Memorandum for the Secretary of State: East-West Institute." NSF Subject File: East-West Institute. Lyndon B. Johnson Presidential Library.

Benson, Etienne S. 2020. *Surroundings: A History of Environments and Environmentalisms*. Chicago: University of Chicago Press.

Bernstein, Steven F. 2001. *The Compromise of Liberal Environmentalism*. New York: Columbia University Press.

Bettencourt, Luis M. A., and Jasleen Kaur. 2011. "Evolution and Structure of Sustainability Science." *PNAS* 108 (49): 19540–45.

Boulding, Kenneth E. 1956. "General Systems Theory: The Skeleton of Science." *Management Science* 2/3 (April): 197–208.

Brandt, Willy, and Independent Commission on International Development Issues. 1980. *North-South : A Programme for Survival: Report of the Independent Commission on International Development Issues*. Cambridge: MIT Press.

58 Caradonna, Jeremy L. 2018. *Routledge Handbook of the History of Sustainability*. London: Routledge.

Clark, William C., and Alicia G. Harley. 2020. "Sustainability Science: Toward a Synthesis." *Annual Review of Environment and Resources* 45 (October): 331–86.

Clark, William C., and Nancy M. Dickson. 2003. "Sustainability Science: The Emerging Research Program." *PNAS* 100 (14): 8059–61.

Foell, Wesley K. 1979. *Management of Energy/Environment Systems: Methods and Case Studies*. Chichester: John Wiley & Sons.

Forrester, Jay W. 1971. *World Dynamics*. Cambridge: Wright-Allen Press.

Gerovitch, Slava. 2002. *From Newspeak to Cyberspeak: A History of Soviet Cybernetics*. Cambridge: MIT Press.

Häfele, Wolf, Jeanne Anderer, Alan McDonald, and Nebojsa Nakicenovic. 1981. *Energy in a Finite World: Paths to a Sustainable Future*. Cambridge: Ballinger Publishing.

Hamblin, Jacob D. 2017. *Arming Mother Nature: The Birth of Catastrophic Environmentalism*. Oxford: Oxford University Press.

Holling, Crawford Stanley, ed. 1978. *Adaptive Environmental Assessment and Management*. Chichester: John Wiley & Sons.

IIASA. 1972. *Charter of the International Institute for Applied Systems Analysis*. Laxenburg, Austria: IIASA.

IUCN, UNEP, WWF. 1980. *World Conservation Strategy: Living Resource Conservation for Sustainable Development*. Gland, Switzerland: IUCN.

Kates, Robert W., William C. Clark, Robert Corell, J. Michael Hall, et al. 2001. "Sustainability Science." *Science* 292 (5517): 641–42.

Kline, Ronald R. 2015. *The Cybernetic Moment: Or Why We Call Our Age the Information Age*. Baltimore: Johns Hopkins University Press.

Kreisky, Bruno. (1984) 1985. *Is There a Chance for a New and Global Detente?* Laxenburg, Austria: IIASA.

Lane, David C., and John D. Sterman. 2011. "Jay Wright Forrester." In *Profiles in Operation Research*, edited by Arjang A. Assad, and Saul I. Gass, 363–86. Boston: Springer.

Leistert, Oliver, and Isabell Schrickel. 2020. *Thinking the Problematic: Genealogies and Explorations Between Philosophy and the Sciences*. Bielefeld: transcript Verlag.

Levien, Roger E. 1967. International Center for the Study of Common Problems of the Industrialized Nations. Grant File PA 73-564. Rockefeller Archive Center, Ford Foundation.

———.1979. "Introduction to IIASA: Applying Systems Analysis in an International Setting." *Systems Research* 24 (3): 155–68.

Levien, Roger E., and M. E. Maron. 1964. *Cybernetics and Its Development in the Soviet Union*. RAND Report: RM-4156-PR. The Rand Corporation.

Lyons, Richard D. 1972. "U.S. and Soviet Will Lead A 12-Nation 'Think Tank'." *New York Times*, October 5, 1972.

Meadows, Donella, John Richardson, and Gerhart Bruckmann. 1982. *Groping in the Dark: The First Decade of Global Modelling*. Chichester: John Wiley & Sons.

Meadows, Donella H., Dennis L. Meadows, Jørgen Randers, and William W. Behrens III. 1972. *The Limits to Growth: A Report for the Club of Rome's Project on the Predicament of Mankind*. New York: Universe Books.

Moll, Peter. 1991. *From Scarcity to Sustainability: Futures Studies and the Environment: the Role of the Club of Rome*. Frankfurt: Peter Lang.

Noble, Michael. 1972. "Dinner Speech at the Occasion of the Plenary Meeting of IIASA." Document CAB 164/1079. British National Archive.

Nordhaus, William D. 1975. "World Modeling from the Bottom Up." IIASA Research Memorandum RM-75-10. IIASA.

Parikh, Kirit, and Ferenc Rabár. 1981. *Food for All in a Sustainable World: The IIASA Food and Agriculture Program*. IIASA Status Report SR-81-002. IIASA.

Raiffa, Howard. 1972. Speech to Members of the US/NAS IIASA Advisory Committee on June 22, 1972. IIASA Archives. IIASA.

Rindzevičiūtė, Egle. 2016. *The Power of Systems: How Policy Sciences Opened Up the Cold War World*. Ithaca: Cornell University Press.

Riska-Campbell, Leena. 2011. *Bridging East and West: The Establishment of the International Institute for Applied Systems Analysis (IIASA) in the United States Foreign Policy of Bridge Building, 1964–1972*. Helsinki: The Finnish Society of Sciences and Letters.

Schrickel, Isabell. 2017. "Control versus Complexity: Approaches to the Carbon Dioxide Problem at IIASA." *Berichte zur Wissenschaftsgeschichte* 40 (2): 140–59.

Scott, Bernard. 2004. "Second-order Cybernetics: An Historical Introduction." *Kybernetes* 33 (9/10): 1365–78.

Sprenger, Florian. 2019. *Epistemologien des Umgebens: Zur Geschichte, Ökologie und Biopolitik künstlicher environments*. Bielefeld: transcript Verlag.

Vieille Blanchard, Elodie. 2010. "Modelling the Future: an Overview of the 'Limits to Growth' Debate." *Centaurus* 52 (2): 91–116.

von Bertalanffy, Ludwig. 1951. "General System Theory: A New Approach to Unity of Science." *Human Biology* 23 (4): 302–12.

———.1968. *General System Theory: Foundations, Development, Applications*. New York: George Braziller.

von Foerster, Heinz. (1991) 2003. "Ethics and Second-Order Cybernetics." In *Understanding Understanding: Essays on Cybernetics and Cognition*, 287–304. New York: Springer-Verlag.

Warde, Paul. 2018. *The Invention of Sustainability: Nature and Destiny, c.1500–1870*. Cambridge: University Press.

Warde, Paul, Libby Robin, and Sverker Sörlin. 2018. *The Environment: The History of an Idea*. Baltimore: John Hopkins University Press.

Warren, P. T. 1972. Dinner Guest List. Document CAB 164/1079. British National Archive.

WCED. 1987. *Our Common Future*. Oxford: Oxford University Press.

Wynne, Brian. 1984. "The Institutional Context of Science, Models, and Policy: The IIASA Energy Study." *Policy Sciences* 17 (3): 277–320.

Zuckerman, Solly, 1972. Memoranda of the IIASA Site Working Group. Document CAB 134/3470. British National Archive.

COMPLEXITY SCIENCE

AGENT-BASED MODELING

SOCIO-CYBERNETICS

REALITY MINING

3

Social Supercolliders: On the Promises and Pitfalls of Grand-Scale Participatory ICT Projects

Sebastian Vehlken

In the wake of the 2008 financial crisis, the FuturICT initiative set out to develop media-technological explanations and solutions for the laws behind complex, global, and socially interactive systems. As a decentralized super-computing project, it aimed to improve social governance, multifaceted risk management, and increasing resilience and responsive-ness in the face of unpredictable crises. From a media-historical perspective, two facets of the FuturICT project are of particular interest: First, its white papers mark a new kind of par-ticipatory, data-driven science that wants to know little of its (social) cybernetic heritage. Moreover, its positivist euphoria about reality

 mining hardly ever reflected on the pitfalls extensively discussed by sociology of risk, which in fact ended a first wave of planning and control in the 1970s. Second, if situated in a broader discursive context of similar ideas about the democratization of Big Data, why did FuturICT's proposal for a third way—beyond Silicon-Valley-style surveillance capitalism and Chinese-style state surveillance—remain unsuccessful?

Today, society and technology are changing at a pace that often outstrips our capacity to understand and manage them. It seems that we know more about the universe than about our society. —Dirk Helbing

Introduction: Flagship Project Makers

With a dramatic tone, in 2010 an international team led by physicist and computational sociologist Dirk Helbing addressed a novel, grand-scale EU research scheme. The *EU Future and Emerging Technologies Flagships projects* were set up, each having one billion euros in funding. Helbing and his collaborators claimed nothing less than creating a "CERN for the social sciences" (Helbing 2013b) and named their brainchild *"FuturICT"*—an acronym for "Future Information and Communication Technologies" (Bishop and Helbing n.d.).

FuturICT took the long shadow of the 2008 global financial crisis as an opportunity to exploit media-technological explanations and solutions for the "invisible laws and processes behind complex, global, and socially-interactive systems of all kinds" (Helbing 2015). The project's concept papers and press releases subsequently merged the physical and sociological genealogies

of the project: the social sciences' CERN was imagined as a hub
that would connect hundreds of researchers from complexity
science, ICT, and social sciences, all across Europe. Furthermore,
its purported search for the underlying laws of a "social physics"
(Pentland 2015) was garnished with a continuing spillover of ever
more creative neologisms like "social supercomputing," "large
knowledge collider," or "living earth simulator" (Ackerman 2010;
Morgan 2010; Bishop and Helbing n.d.).

In a nutshell, the project's goal was to integrate multiple networking, simulation, and visualization technologies in order to
bring knowledge about socio-political, socio-economic, and infra-
structural systems into the "public domain." Facilitated by proposed regional data observatories, participatory access became
a primary issue. Similarly, the creation of a "democratic version"
of Big Data was key. Data from diverse sources—e.g., from
weather forecasts to social networks, or from health databases
to traffic monitoring—were to be "mined" outside of the logic
of platform capitalism and Big Tech companies (Helbing and
Balietti 2011a; Bishop and Helbing n.d.). Instead, *FuturICT*'s social
supercomputing aimed to improve social control, multifaceted
risk management, and increasing responsiveness in the face of
unforeseeable crises.

These propositions were based on a set of "innovative"
technologies centered, above all, on Agent-Based Models
(ABMs) and computer simulations. Or, in Helbing's words, they
were grounded in "socially inspired paradigms" for ICT (Helbing
2012). Retrospectively however, despite its discourse on participation and democratic accessibility, *FutureICT* was unable
to avoid common negative connotations associated with
computerized governments—ranging from inhumane technocracy
to surveillance operations. Consequently, most readers may
have never heard of *FuturICT*: whereas the initiative succeeded in
reaching the selection round of the last six Flagship projects, and
briefly made it into the news headlines (Morgan 2010; Ackerman

64   2010), two competing projects secured the funding instead in 2013.

FuturICT thus became a rather unusual object of research: it turned into an archive of a past future, hosted under a past projects subdomain of the ETH Zurich's website. Thereby, it meets the double-edged etymological root of the term *project* underscored by media historian Markus Krajewski (2004). Deriving from the Latin projectus—i.e., "thrown down, discarded"—the word also has "a resigning component." According to Krajewski, "in the designation 'project,' failure is already etymologically anchored" (Krajewski 2004, 11). On the *"Past Projects"* web page of ETH Zurich, this failure is digitally available in all its glory. Today, *FuturICT* is above all a conglomerate of beginnings, sketches, buzzwords, and potential formulations. Its materiality consists of white papers, draft sketches, science PR films, half-dead links to mind-map-like slides, and, last but not least, several appearances by project leaders at TED conferences, or television shows. In contrast, it also provides substantial research articles, including publications in *Science* and *Nature*, mainly from the field of complexity science (Schich et al. 2014; Brockmann and Helbing 2013; Helbing 2013a).

This material testifies to the past future of a project that dedicated itself to the media-technical anticipation of future crises, without ever being allowed to thematize its own state of crisis. The *Future and Emerging Technologies Flagships* thus take the epistemological character of *projecting* to the extreme: to return to Krajewski, *carrying out projects* (*projektemachen*) involves a project-maker who

> is in a peculiar state of limbo, he operates in the epistemological in-between of an unsecured order and of canonized knowledge. His position marks the transition between a critical predicament and an undecided future to be shaped. His self-appointed task is to assert the

> unthinkable in order to make the impossible realizable. (Krajewski 2004, 24)

This stage, at best, proves to be slippery. All the *FuturICT* remainders tell stories about the multifaceted frictions inherent not only in academic funding processes, but, even more so, in the conceptualization and development of applications for the computational tools of "evidence-based" decision making. From a media-historical perspective, *FuturICT* boils down to a telling tale regarding the "insurmountable opportunities" which separate particle physics from "social physics." Furthermore, it teaches a lesson on the past, present, and future of the materialities of (post-) cybernetic socio-technical systems. And finally, in the light of more recent experiences regarding the implementation of ICT systems for socio-economic analysis and the *forecast* of systemic behaviors, *FuturICT* speaks to the inevitable frictions that come into play for the simple reason that such systems are intrinsically political. They are based on a particular understanding of collective organization, and they each propose a "technological solutionism" (Morozov 2013) for an effective management of their respective (computerized) models of society.

Accordingly, this chapter scrutinizes the promises and pitfalls of *social computing* and ICT initiatives under three main aspects. First, it highlights the frictions between the complexity science mindset of *FuturICT* and earlier approaches to self-organization. Second, it discusses reasons for the continued failure of such approaches—despite the changing technical conditions—and addresses the frictions that emerge at the boundary of decision preparation and decision-making. In a concluding third step, it asks for perspectives that, once again, suggest different strategies of combining data-driven knowledge production, and a supposed societal advancement.

A New Kind of Science

Dirk Helbing, *FuturICT's* prospective principal investigator and mastermind, not only displays an astonishing record of highly-ranked journal papers, but also an ongoing optimism regarding the potentials of digital media to improve our world. Along with other leading German figures of the simulation paradigm, such as Kai Nagel or Michael Schreckenberg, Helbing started to deal with the "physics of socio-economic systems" in the 1990s—e.g., by co-founding the corresponding section in the German Physical Society (DPG 2022). Initially, his research mainly concentrated on logistical systems like traffic networks, or pedestrian and crowd dynamics. Before joining ETH in 2007 as head of the Institute for Computational Sociology, Helbing led the *Transport and Economy* department at TU Dresden. In part, this career path may explain his specific approach to socio-economic phenomena, whereby he seeks quantifiable and formalizable regularities in collective behaviors which apply to human, animal, and inanimate multi-particle physical systems alike.

> In the past, it was impossible to experiment with our future. This made social sciences different from the natural and engineering sciences, in which different options can be tried out before choosing one. In the future, we will also be able to make experiments with different socioeconomic designs. (Helbing and Balietti 2011b, 85)

According to Helbing's own reports, the need for other ICT-supported methods of organization arose shortly before the outbreak of the financial crisis in 2008.

> Most people expected that the problems in the US real estate market and the banking system could be fixed. However, it was already clear to me and also to many other complexity scientists that they would cause cascade effects … At that time, I said that nobody understood our financial system, our economy, and our society well enough to grasp the related problems and to manage them successfully.

> Therefore, I proposed to invest into a large-scale project in
> the social sciences—including economics ... I stressed that
> ... we would require a "knowledge accelerator" to keep up
> with the pace at which our societies are faced with emerging
> problems. (Helbing 2015, 2)

This formulation was addressed a little later with a first large-scale project called Visioneer, conducted between 2009 and 2010.

> Visioneer was a European project aiming to reach a better,
> quantitative understanding of complex socio-economic
> systems. The ultimate purpose was to develop the concept
> of a Social Knowledge Collider, thereby creating optimal
> conditions to unleash the potential of real multi-disciplinary
> projects involving social scientists, economists, computer
> scientists, physicists, biologists, system scientists, and
> engineers. (Helbing 2015, 3–4)

The *Knowledge Collider* remained the guiding metaphor for the subsequent *FuturICT* project. By 2013, it had grown into a broad network of hundreds of institutions and individuals. Additionally, 90 million euros in third-party funding had been raised. Then, *FuturICT* boldly stated the beginning of a new science:

> Neither the precepts of traditional science, nor our collective
> experience from a simpler past, adequately prepare us for
> the future. It is simply impossible to understand and manage
> complex networks using conventional tools. We need to
> put systems in place that highlight, or prevent, conceivable
> failures and allow us to quickly recover from those that we
> cannot predict. (Bishop and Helbing n.d.)

Risks and crises of all kinds should be subjected to permanent ICT management—financial markets as well as epidemics, social instabilities, or criminal networks (Bishop and Helbing n.d.). Away from the processing of system components and their properties, with their interactions becoming the focus instead, risk and the crises themselves should become modulable. In other words, when the (mis)behaviors of systems come to the fore, their cascading effects can be countered with the help of computer and media technology *management systems.*

Historical Genealogies

Similar diagnoses of overwhelming crises are permanent companions of the development of modern societies—be it industrialized metropolitan life at the turn of the 20th century, or the early discourse of computerization and automation in the long 1970s. Thus, the foundations of *FuturICT* can be better situated by placing them in relation to the epoch of cybernetics, where a specific techno-informational mode of regulation was extended to socio-economic domains in order to develop a "behavioral science of systems." From the beginning, cybernetics formulated universal, information-theoretical descriptions of communication and control. There, behavior becomes describable not only by means of a new, technical vocabulary, but rather as a problem category that concerns the technical settings of increasingly complex information machines. These systems continue to be used, in historically different ways, to gain insights into other complex systems and their behaviors.

Cybernetics understood complexity as a property in its own right. Systems and their (dis-)functionalities were abstracted from real-life situations in the form of analog or digital models, and became explorable *as* such. Accordingly, they were transferred between different subject areas in an interdisciplinary way, becoming the starting point for the formulation of general theories about systems behavior (McLoughlin and Webster 1970). Thus, computer-technical investigations into systems behavior understood that the transmission, processing, and storage operations of digital technologies were part of a "behavioral science of systems" (Mahr 2003). In that context, (re)producing systems behavior as realistically as possible, it is less about system conformity than about a range of *tweaking practices* and modifiable models. Therefore, the generated knowledge about simulated systems is intrinsically intertwined with the behavior of the simulation systems themselves.

Every form of behavior requires a process of goal-setting in which the necessity of an operationalization of the future is always already inscribed. Not coincidentally, *prediction* became a central catchword in the realm of systems theory and cybernetics—an operation that was only more precise, the larger the processed data sets were. Systems simulate possible errors and thus potential improvements in order to promptly calculate—and this is where it then used to fail—the most probable path (Wiener 1964). Hence, when cybernetics implemented future behavior (in the singular) to guarantee the survival of a system in a changing environment, the necessity of powerful computing facilities and computer simulations anticipated the processing of future systems behaviors (in the plural).

Warren Weaver called such systems "problems of organized complexity"—a class of problems that, with their character- istic property of multiple, interconnected variables, he situated between mundane and predictable "problems of simplicity"— e.g., Newtonian mechanics, "problems of disorganized com- plexity," and motions of gasses or elementary particles that can only be described in more probabilistic terms (Monchaux 2016, 132). Moreover, Weaver saw the quantification and computer- aided cybernetic exploitation of these systems as being well within reach (Monchaux 2016, 132). This is what made cybernetic models for multivariable systems attractive in the 1960s. They were employed in fields such as economics and business admin- istration, in urban planning and development, and even—as shown by the much-cited, but precipitously failed case of Stafford Beer's Project *Cybersyn* in Chile—as media of governance (Medina 2011).

Perhaps, cybernetics' universalist regulatory undertaking reveals itself most clearly in the models developed by Jay W. Forrester

 and his group at MIT. In a similar framework, he began modeling
Industrial Dynamics, then moved onto *Urban Dynamics*, before
climaxing with the famous *World Dynamics* model for the Club
of Rome (Forrester 1961; 1964; 1973; Meadows et al. 1972) where
notions of cybernetic homeostasis took on planetary proportions
(Lovelock and Margulis 1974). However, these simulations—often
under the umbrella term of *systems dynamics*—turned out to
be as limited as their social statistical predecessors, whose
bureaucratic apparatuses and slow modes of response they
had promised to replace (Hacking 1990; 2006). The multitude of
operators and feedback loops populating Forrester's diagrams
led to over-simplifications, abstractions, and biases that they had
actually set out to remedy. The reason for this was a consistent
lack of usable data—sometimes with disastrous consequences.
In 1974 for example, there was a network of fire stations that had
previously been systematically downsized on the basis of model
calculations by the RAND Corporation. This downsizing was
seen as being to blame for the catastrophic scale of a series of
major fires in the Bronx (Monchaux 2016, 134). Similarly, unfore-
seen events such as the oil crises of the 1970s brought about a
period of disillusionment with the paradigms of cybernetic communication and control, extinguishing the previously widespread
"planning euphoria" (Seefried 2015, 411). The highly abstracted
and simplified models of systems dynamics and other similar
approaches, which attempted a *formal* and functional simulation
of real-world phenomena, failed to do justice to their real complex behaviors.

More Is Different

However, new mathematical models and simulations, also related
to systems behavior, emerged in other contexts. In 1972, physicist
Philip W. Anderson, who at Bell Labs had long been involved
in thought related to cybernetic systems behavior, succinctly
summarized its epistemological pitfalls without getting lost in
meta discourse. His text *"More Is Different,"* published in *Science,*

focuses on the effects and irreducibility of nonlinear processes
in the behavior of multivariable systems: "The ability to reduce
everything to simple fundamental laws does not imply the ability
to start from those laws and reconstruct the universe" (Anderson
1972, 393). Complex systems are characterized by the production
of emergent properties, which cannot be derived from the properties of the initial configuration of the system. They emerged
only in its procedural course, through the manifold interactions
of individual system components. Thus, the construction of
control schematics for the interaction flows within a system was
no longer at issue. Rather, modeling interest shifted to system
behaviors that resulted directly from the disaggregated micro-
behaviors of the elements of the system.

Compared to the "age of cybernetics" (Pias 2004) the research of
complexity science fundamentally changed the perspective on
systems behavior. In simulation models such as *systems dynamics*,
the constituents of the system to be modeled were grouped
into a set of subsystems that could interact with each other in
a variety of exchange relationships. This required, however, a
certain amount of prior knowledge, which severely limited the
possible interactions within the system—where a system was
essentially treated as a message engineering problem, anything
that could not be interpreted as such was simply left out.

In complexity science, modeling was transformed into bottom-
up methods, which start with the interactions of the smallest
components of the system—e.g., between proteins in molecular
biology, birds flocking together, or the "millions of mutually interdependent individuals who make up a human society" (Waldrop
1992, 11). In such systems, novel collective behavior is derived
from local interactions, which is reflected in the spontaneous
formation of specific temporal, spatial, and functional structures.
Where cybernetics had previously searched for universal
switching schemes, complexity science now searches for the
constituent properties of the autonomous formation of patterns,

 and the ordering processes of the dynamic and unpredictable behaviors of a system.

In contrast to early cybernetics, complexity theories are not developed in dialogue with experimental machine models, but with computer applications like cellular automata (Wolfram 2002), and by means of new programming methods such as genetic or evolutionary algorithms (Holland 1992). If cybernetics aimed to define control mechanisms that guaranteed a constant dynamic equilibrium of a system, these theories are interested in the exact opposite: behind much of the relevant research there are questions about critical transition points in the organization of systems.

The fascination of complexity science was generated by the hope of building a new bridge between the two cultures of natural sciences on one hand, and humanities and social sciences on the other. Mathematical-computational research of emergent system behavior and self-organization phenomena could be applied in a much more versatile way to the description of real-world problems—e.g., from climate and earthquake predictions to stock market dynamics, or from traffic systems to epidemics, or to processes of opinion-forming in a society (Meyers 2009, v). In this context, the expectancy of developing informative simu-lation models for whole societies—i.e. a *Generative Social Science* (Epstein 2006)—had also been formulated, which in turn found reverberation in *FuturICT*. These possibilities can be interpreted as a direct consequence of the developments on computation:

> The science of complex systems is unthinkable without computers. The analytical tools available until the 1980s were good enough to address problems based on dif-ferential equations, for systems in equilibrium, for linear (or sufficiently linearizable) systems, and for stochastic systems with weak interactions. The problems associated with evolutionary processes, non-ergodicity, out-of-equilibrium systems, self-organization, path dependence, and so on,

were practically beyond scientific reach, mainly because of computational limits. (Thurner, Hanel, and Klimek 2018, 16)

In contrast to the undertaking of cybernetics, a structural coupling between real-world phenomena, models, and simulations of complexity science now seems possible. It is just this *structural* coupling which carries an inherent possibility of building bridges between *FuturICT*'s crisis-ridden problem areas, and pithy slogans such as a "Large Knowledge Collider" and a "CERN for the Social Sciences." Enriched by all kinds of data feeds from the systems to be modeled, they can be seen as the media technologies that set the stage for our contemporary "smartness mandate"—i.e., the assertion that any kind of relationship between people, their technologies, and their environments can and should be managed algorithmically (Halpern, Mitchell, and Geoghegan 2017, 119).

Black Hole Sons

Three components stand out in *FuturICT*'s planning papers, especially since they are labeled using training buzzwords and rhetoric around proposals: the *Planetary Nervous System,* the *Living Earth Simulator,* and the *Global Participatory Platform.* The *Planetary Nervous System* can be thought of as a global network of sensors, where sensors include anything that can provide static and dynamic data about socioeconomic, ecological, or technological systems. Such infrastructure would enable real-time data mining—"Reality Mining" (Bishop and Helbing n.d.)—by using data from online surveys, lab experiments, the semantic web, or smartphone sensors, in turn providing aggregated information. Among the goals was to create more meaningful indices than mere statistical ones such as GDP, taking into account social, environmental, and health factors. To encourage users to voluntarily provide their data, a system of incentives and micropayments would be developed, allowing people to control their own data and privacy.

 Embedded in the Big Data discourse that took off around 2010 (Anderson 2008; Boyd and Crawford 2012), "reality" is conceptualized here as essentially data-driven. *FutureICT* hoped that its large-scale structural analysis could make it possible to describe socio-economic systems from a scientific perspective, contrasting with the marketing perspective pushed by Big Tech companies. This would serve a better understanding of collective dynamics through larger data sets, refine social and cognitive behavioral models, and thus foster the preparation of social and individual response strategies to future problems (Helbing and Balietti 2011b).

Although they formed part of the hype around Big Data, *FuturICT*'s white papers also show an awareness of the dangers of Big Data analytics from the outset—which was all but self-evident in the discourse of the time. Ethical and legal problems were discussed extensively, and a combination of data-driven approaches with complementary human intuition, experimental approaches, or computer simulations were proposed when dealing with Big Data:

> Large datasets support the temptation to perform "blind" data mining, i.e. to apply pattern recognition tools and statistical methods without a deeper understanding of the underlying assumptions and implications of the results … Typical problems are: 1. (mis-) interpreting correlations as causal relationships, 2. collinearity of variables … 3. underfitting or overfitting of mathematical models, 4. ignorance of underlying simplifications or critical approximations, 5. … the illusion of control over complex systems. This is quite dangerous and probably what happened during the recent financial crisis. (Helbing and Balietti 2011a, 13)

The *Living Earth Simulator* was the key concept for the exploration of future scenarios. It should have integrated heterogeneous data, and have employed a variety of theoretical and modeling perspectives, such as agent-based simulations and mathematical

models, as well as new empirical and experimental approaches.
Likewise, inputs from complexity science would be assessed
with graph theory and other techniques from statistical physics,
thanks to the support of a "World of Modeling": an open-source
platform to which scientists and developers would be able to
upload modeling components which were informed by theory
and empirically validated. This required, therefore, the development of interactive, decentralized, and scalable computing
infrastructures with access to vast amounts of data. Put differently, supercomputing capabilities which would be provided—
the project-makers hoped—by several leading European centers
(Bishop and Helbing n.d.).

This certainly speaks of a positivist approach not only regarding
the world, but also the computational tools that would model
it—tools into which everything that is perceivable would simply
be shoved. This points to a certain arrogance in *FuturICT*'s proposal; not only concerning its conceptual side, but also its actual
feasibility. A dispassionate look at the complexities implicit in
far more modest initiatives—for instance, the German National
Research Data Infrastructure (NFDI)—may quickly demonstrate
the scale of the efforts and timeframes required to realize even
a fraction of what *FuturICT* aimed to. This arrogance, however,
was perhaps simply incited by the funding scheme. In any case,
FuturICT did not stop there. Similarly to the data centers of
globally active Internet service providers, it aimed to enable a
high evaluation speed by better linking the storage and processing of data—particularly through applications like *Apache Hadoop*
(White 2009). This plethora of information, then, was to be
adjusted to facilitate public availability and *democratization*.

The *Global Participatory Platform* was meant to be an open framework for citizens, businesses, and organizations, aiming to share,
explore, and discuss the potential impact of data and simulations.
It was conceptualized as a medium to democratize Big Data, promote responsible use of information systems, and open up the
modeling of complex systems to non-experts. Helbing sensibly

 summarizes this as a shift in perspective that takes operations rooms away from the tradition of war rooms, by rethinking and reenacting them as "peace rooms" (Helbing and Seele 2017). These "Decision Arenas" were planned for policymakers to assess the consequences of interventions (Helbing and Balietti 2011b, 18), then to be opened up and tailored to the needs of different stakeholders.

This was supposed, first, to enable software developers to add value to the platform—e.g., mobile applications that use or upload data. Second, the platform's core idea was to serve the development of visualization tools—e.g., for policy analysts, citizens, and researchers. Third, it was meant to foster the development of semantic web services for distributed e-science platforms in terms of reflective, participatory online debates. The resulting "world pictures" (Heidegger 1977) would be brought together in crisis monitoring facilities for focal areas—e.g., finance and economics, crime, conflicts between states, social crises, transportation and logistics, health and the spread of disease, and environmental change.

> "What makes the data Big is repeated observations over time and/or space." Accordingly, there is a need—as a further development of existing applications—for comprehensive visualization tools that provide both an overview and zoom and filter functions for the data. They would have to allow access to selected details—a cooperation of experts for scientific visualizations with graphic designers, artists and communication experts would be highly appropriate here. And an additional democratic component should not be forgotten, to study data in a distributed way from different individual perspectives, namely share. (Jacobs 2009, 40; Helbing and Balietti 2011b, 22; only first line by first author)

This sounds almost like Stafford Beer and Project *Cybersyn*—just as the vision for "Decision Arenas" does:

Combining suitable data, models and visualizations tools,
the final goal would be to develop a virtual observatory of
social, economic and financial systems with the possibility
to explore new scenarios and systems designs through
what is sometimes called a "policy wind tunnel". The corresponding ICT systems should be suited to craft policy
options, contingency plans, and intelligent responses to
emerging challenges and risks. They will allow one to develop
concepts and institutional designs for a flexible, adaptive,
and resource-efficient real-time management of complex
socio-economic systems and organizations. Decision arenas
visualizing, animating, and illustrating the acquired scientific
insights will provide valuable decision-support to decision-
makers, as they will make counter-intuitive feedback, cascading and side effects understandable. (Helbing and Balietti
2011b, 18)

The persistence of *FuturICT*'s white papers on a solution-oriented
rhetoric with regard to digital network technologies is reminiscent
of popular technology-driven smart city dreams, but at the level
of world government—somehow analogous to Jay Forrester's
cybernetic models. This faith in the positive (and positivist) world
design, and in the potentials of digital technologies of course
had to exclude critical diagnoses such as those of media scholar
Wendy Chun, who points out that the relationship between digital
media technologies and crises is thoroughly ambivalent:

Codes, historically linked to rules and laws, seek to exempt
us from hurt or injury by establishing norms, which order
the present and render calculable the future ... Tellingly,
trusted computer systems are systems secure from user
intervention and understanding. Moreover, software codes
not only save the future by restricting user action, they also
do so by drawing on saved data and analysis. They are, after
all, programmed. They thus seek to free us from danger by
reducing the future to the past, or, more precisely, to a past
anticipation of the future. Remarkably, though, computer

systems have been linked to user empowerment and agency, as much as they have been condemned as new forms of control. Still more remarkably, software codes have not simply reduced crises, they have also proliferated them. From financial crises linked to complex software programs to super-computer dependent diagnoses and predictions of global climate change, from undetected computer viruses to bombings at securitized airports, we are increasingly called on both to trust coded systems and to prepare for events that elude them. (Chun 2011, 91–92)

It is precisely this ambivalence that dooms to failure any kind of *socioscope* or policy wind tunnel. It is here that the frictions arise, causing the Large Knowledge Collider to implode. For, in contrast to that meme-rich concern about the creation of a black hole by CERN (Rössler 2008), the black hole of this social supercollider seems to only yawn in its conceptual center.

Frictions in the Black Hole

The effort to present *FutureICT* as an integrative, distributive, and participatory architecture is evidently an effort to refute any accusations of technocracy from the outset. Despite bold slogans, those involved in the project can by no means be accused of conceptual under-reflection. Due to the transdisciplinary disposition of the project, a multitude of critical objections against the proposed practices of data mining had already been extensively formulated in the white papers and in comment sections of special journal issues that prepared the field for *FuturICT* (Allen 2011; Thurner 2011). It seems that a media and cultural studies critique was internally implemented, seeking to anticipate any reservation. Beyond the display of self-criticism, it would therefore be more appropriate to ask what value these statements actually had for the *FutureICT* project. After all, the white papers cited here not only offer an extensive collection of material on social simulations, but also clever rhetoric around

funding applications. Accordingly, the impression arises that the
implementation of self-criticism leads to a number of loose ends.

First, the application does not emphasize the narrow scope
for this type of project in view of the existing but inadequate
instruments of "socio-economic management." Neither is there
an open reference to the critique of progress. Conversely, existing
problems, like the "mining" and processing of relevant data, are
simply transferred to the development of the project as promises
of future solutions. However, the constant allusion to the new
possibilities of digitally networked societies refers only to one of
the sides pointed out by Chun—i.e., the emancipatory potential of
decentralized networks. This is especially relevant since *FuturICT*
also intended to gain control over the protocols that were supposed to make these media democratic (Galloway 2004). We
should keep in mind, nonetheless, that *FuturICT* was formulated
before acronyms like PRISM[1] or GCHQ[2] became part of the public
discussion, and before the idea emerged that communication
networks might not automatically generate connecting capacities,
but also socially disintegrating ones. Put differently, a *Planetary
Nervous System* can suffer from strong nervous convulsions, as
the last decade of regression has shown (Pörksen 2018; Reckwitz
2019; Appadurai et al. 2017).

Second, although Helbing and others in the team expose the
inadequacies of classical economic models, they do this only
by focusing themselves on the limitations of the *homo economicus* model, which they contrast with the figure of a *homo
socialis*—the latter acting cooperatively rather than selfishly.
Similar to Robert Axelrod's (1984) studies on the evolution of
cooperation, this approach is based on simulation programs with
physics-based parameterizations. In the context of his original

1   An NSA intelligence program surveying communications exchanges from
     several US Internet companies.
2   The British Government Communications Headquarters, an intelligence
     agency similar to the NSA.

 field of expertise—evacuation and panic research—Helbing had investigated the behavior of crowds in the context of catastrophes. Then, he described the "freezing-by-heating effect" (Helbing, Farkas, and Vicsek 2000) and the "slower-is-faster paradox" (Helbing and Mazloumian 2009)—both phenomena in which faster individual movements in crowds lead to macroscopic stalling effects, while cooperative behavior produces much better results. Here, however, the *homo socialis* is problematized through *frictions* between individuals which are primarily thought of in terms of physical frictions, without having semantic levels in mind.

Thirdly, this connects to a systemic incoherence concerning the decision-making process. On one hand, models based mainly on rational actors, such as *homo economicus*, were taken as an opportunity to alternatively design more complex, *data-based*, and heterogeneous models. However, in dealing with the data generated by *FuturICT*, the next step would be precisely to appeal to such rationalistically understood *decision-makers*, who would be able to implement *better, more intelligent,* or *more adequate* decisions. The fact that this translation of expert knowledge into political action could become problematic is deliberately concealed in the white papers.

Fourth, defying the break with cybernetic approaches described above, a universalist ideal pervades the distributive network plans of *FuturICT*. Perhaps the greatest fallacy of both earlier cybernetic designs and complexity science, these social super-colliders—announcing an overarching conceptual setting of cybernetic feedback systems, social physics, and capture-all data—claim ubiquitous validity for all aspects and domains. At *FuturICT*, the get-the-right-data problem of previous decades morphed into the familiar Big Data mantra *"get the data right."* Thus, the conviction remains that an overarching communication and control system can and should be implemented. Therefore, regardless of all rhetorical anticipation of technocratic accusations, old qualms also endure: as with *Cybersyn,* universalist systems run the permanent risk of becoming exactly the opposite of what they were intended to be.

Fifth, this may be connected to the lack of reflection on the relationship between science and politics. The structural incompatibility of such a bond was summed up by none other than Hannah Arendt in her essay *"Truth and Politics"* (1967). Accordingly, the insistence on computationally expanding the horizons for decision-making and data-driven knowledge processes falls short when data become facts. After all, a common characteristic of political action is not to do what would be rationally opportune in the long or medium term. Reformulated in a rather Luhmannian (1994) manner: because of their functional difference, science, society, and politics will each treat *data* very differently, so that in each area quite different *facts* will be derived from the same data. This, however, is only recognized by those who do not equate *data* with *facts* (Rosenberg 2013), and decision preparations—i.e., science—with actual decisions—i.e., politics (Luhmann 2000). The experience from recent years—e.g., in the area of pandemic simulation—has shown that data-based decision-making, while offering immense advantages, often blurs the lines of conflict in decision-making processes: what amount of the epidemiologically-quantified index for distancing measures do I sacrifice in relation to the economically-quantified index for maintaining production processes? It does make a difference to how complex social systems are understood and modeled, as well as how this knowledge is communicated to the society, and thus effectively implemented (Priesemann et al. 2021). If one includes the unpredictability of daily global politics in this picture, it may become apparent that beneath this "Large Knowledge Collider" the aforementioned black hole lurks—under whose gravity all possible futures are stretched beyond recognition.

A sixth objection refers to the Agent-Based Simulation paradigm. What works very well for traffic or pedestrian systems, reaches its limits in the context of more complex social systems. As David O'Sullivan and Mordechai Haklay (2000) pointed out, the individual-based approach of these models only considers partial aspects—a bias that neglects the role of institutions and other social organizations as part of a mid-level between individuals and global structures. Hence, these models show an inadequacy similar to that pointed out by Herbert Simon regarding market-radical positions. Only having transactions in mind, they would not have planned structures thoroughly, leaving firms and other organizations adrift (Simon 1983). This could be extended to the vision of distributed, grassroots co-decision-making in peace rooms. Certainly, *FuturICT* was a contemporary of the German Pirate Party and initiatives such as Liquid Democracy (Ramos 2015). Political opinion, however, or even culture, are not just functions of interactions based on a few rules. Long-running discussions suggest how complex the topic of participation is in the context of digital technologies (Denecke et al. 2016; Center for Digital Participation n.d.)—and that it will not be enough to adopt a technology-driven approach, like the so-called *peace rooms*.

Seventh, computer simulations raise a fundamental epistemological problem, which, according to Wendy Chun, refers to programs and trust:

> That is, "trusting" a program does not mean letting it decide the future or even framing its future predictions as simply true, but instead acknowledging the impossibility of knowing its truth in advance while nonetheless responding to it. This is perhaps made most clear through the example of global climate models, which attempt to convince people that something they can't yet experience, something simulated, is true. (Chun 2011, 106–07)

This resonates with *FuturICT* and the irresolvable circular argument that social systems react differently than climate to the predictions of their behavior, thus making them immediately invalid again. In the words of economist Alex Tabarrok: "The problem of perfectly organizing an economy does not become easier with greater computing power precisely because greater

computing power also makes the economy more complex"
(Tabarrok 2018). It could be argued that the most striking pitfall
of *FuturICT* lies in its focus on providing solutions for complex
societal problems and developing the necessary infrastructures
at once. Put differently, despite its legacy of complexity studies,
there still seems to be a residual *systems dynamics* mindset there.

Helbing's grim complaint after the Flagship's decision against
FuturICT may put this in perspective:

> While the project was doing impressively well, to everyone's
> surprise it was finally not funded, even though we pro-
> posed an approach aiming at ethical information and com-
> munication technologies, with a focus on privacy and citizen
> participation. This possibly meant that governments had
> decided against *FuturICT*'s open, transparent, participatory,
> and privacy-respecting approach, and that they might invest
> in secret projects instead. (Helbing 2015, 3)

Indeed, the Snowden revelations may have somehow reinforced
this claim. However, the critical aspects discussed above offer
more realistic reasons for the project failing to receive funding.

Beware the Borg

In late 2019, *The Economist* devoted an extensive article to possible futures and the viability of various models of data capitalism. Under the original title *"Beware the Borg,"* it thoroughly
reflected on the historical genealogies of the current developments, taking operations rooms, and *Project Cybersyn* in
particular, as the starting point for a wide-ranging discussion on
the antagonisms between market-based and planned economics
since the 1920s—discussions that would have led to new hybrid
forms such as AI-thoritarianism and infrastructures saturated by
machine learning (The Economist 2019). As a discarded project
that did not emphasize AI aspects, *FuturICT* did not play a role
in the article. Nevertheless, almost a decade after the start of

    this project, the article once again framed questions from that time within a bigger picture. China's social credit systems are discussed alongside social media infowars, and the erosion of democratic societies in a Western surveillance-based economy (The Economist 2019). Similarly to Zuboff (2019), in these cases "information-machine-like" cultures of control, predictability, and automation of processes propagate from the private sphere to the societal level. The focus is thus on the "dark side of the digital," and the question about viable alternative models is raised. Consequently, the central point of the article is turning away from the "thoughtlessness" of media-technical automation and algorithmization, towards a "thoughtfulness" in multi-stage decision-making processes:

> If planners—or regulators, for that matter—want to intervene in something, it is with the platform that they are best advised to start. It is the place where code becomes law, where the mechanisms by which a market works are specified …

> … This way of thinking of things allows a new insight into the calculation debate. In treating both the planning system and the market as what might now be called computer programs it made them comparable. Take the next step of seeing the type of program … as a platform, though, and they become very different …

> Platforms are already a source of huge and increasing power, commercial and otherwise. Politics needs to catch up with this, not just in terms of regulating commerce—where the issue is already a hot one—but also by opening up discussion of the values that platforms embody and encourage. (The Economist 2019)

However, the merging of different participatory platforms is precisely what must be avoided. Instead, a platform world that is as pluralistic as possible should be embraced:

> Some basic platforms, such as digital identity and digital currency, perhaps, should probably be owned by governments, or at the very least open to policing by them. Other platforms need to allow oversight by their users and civil society to ensure an absence of bias ... and privacy infringements. (The Economist 2019)

Such proposals do not seem far removed from the approach formulated by *FuturICT*. In their emphasis on variety however, these proposals do not claim to bring together all disparities for the purpose of a more efficient planning, or for the development of concrete technologies. Moreover, they are not the brainchild of an academic funding structure whose authority for redefining political conditions must always be contestable. Conversely, approaches like Francesca Bria's "Big Democracy" resonate here (Monge et al. 2022; Morozov and Bria 2018). Alongside fellow campaigners such as urban planner Carlos Moreno, Bria—a former digital expert for the city of Barcelona—takes traditional ideas of smart cities as a starting point to redefine livable cities in the age of ubiquitous digital technologies (Monge et al. 2022; Moreno 2020). With attention to concrete places and human experiences, broader notions for digital futures are sketched out; where Big Democracy becomes the European answer to Big Tech from the US, and China's Big State. In contrast to *FuturICT* however, here politics does not degenerate into a mere function of digital infrastructures, but is rather a prerequisite for them. To return to Wendy Chun:

> What can emerge positively from the linking of crisis to networks—what must emerge from it if we are not to exhaust ourselves and our resources—are constant ethical encounters between self and other. These moments can call forth a new future, a way to exhaust exhaustion, even as they complicate the deconstructive promise of responsibility (Chun 2011, 107).

This *"new future"* may well emerge from multiple initiatives, rather than from a unifying academic research proposal; it might be rooted in concrete locations like cities, with connections to tangible living environments, rather than being the product of abstract network approaches. After all, the larger part of social super-collisions still happens on the streets.

References

Ackerman, Evan. 2010. "Living Earth Simulator Will Predict the Future of Everything." *Dvice* (extinct online magazine). Accessed July 5, 2014. http://www.dvice.com/archives/2010/12/living_earth_si.php.

Allen, Peter. 2011. "Comments by P. Allen on the Visioneer white papers by D. Helbing and S. Balietti." *European Physics Journal—Special Topics* 195 (2011): 137–43. https://doi.org/10.1140/epjst/e2011-01404-5.

Anderson, Chris. 2008. "The End of Theory: The Data Deluge Makes the Scientific Method Obsolete." *Wired*, June 23, 2008. https://www.wired.com/2008/06/pb-theory/.

Anderson, Paul. 1972. "More is Different." *Science* 177 (4047): 393–96. https://doi.org/10.1126/science.177.4047.393.

Appadurai, Arjun, Zygmunt Bauman, Donatella della Porta, Nancy Fraser, et al. 2017. *Die große Regression*. Frankfurt: Suhrkamp.

Arendt, Hannah. 1967. "Truth and Politics." *The New Yorker*, February 25, 1967.

Axelrod, Robert. 1984. *The Evolution of Cooperation*. New York: Basic Books.

Bishop, Steven, and Dirk Helbing. n.d. "FuturICT Project Summary." *FuturICT*. Accessed December 12, 2022. https://futurict.inn.ac/wp-content/uploads/2015/06/FuturICT_5p_Project-Summary-WITH-LOGOS.pdf.

Boyd, Danah, and Kate Crawford. 2012. "Critical Questions for Big Data." *Information, Communication & Society* 15 (5): 662–79. https://doi.org/10.1080/1369118X.2012.678878.

Brockmann, Dirk, and Dirk Helbing. 2013. "The Hidden Geometry of Complex, Network-Driven Contagion Phenomena." *Science* 342 (6164): 1337–42. https://doi.org/10.1126/science.1245200.

Center for Digital Participation. n.d. "CDP: CDP." Accessed December 20, 2022. https://www.digital-participation.org.

Chun, Wendy Hui Kyong. 2011. "Crisis, Crisis, Crisis, or Sovereignty and Networks." *Theory, Culture & Society* 28 (6): 91–112. https://doi.org/10.1177/0263276411418490.

Denecke, Mathias, Anne Ganzert, Isabell Otto, and Robert Stock, eds. 2016. *ReClaiming Participation: Technology—Mediation—Collectivity*. Bielefeld: transcript.

DPG. 2022. "Physics of Socio-economic Systems (SOE)." *DPG*. Accessed December 12, 2022. https://www.dpg-physik.de/vereinigungen/fachlich/skm/fvsoe.

The Economist. 2019. "Can Technology Plan Economies and Destroy Democracy?" *The Economist*, December 18, 2019. https://www.economist.com/christmas-specials/2019/12/18/can-technology-plan-economies-and-destroy-democracy.

Epstein, Joshua M. 2006. *Generative Social Science: Studies in Agent-Based Computational Modeling*. Princeton: Princeton University Press.

Forrester, Jay Wright. 1961. *Industrial Dynamics*. Cambridge: MIT Press.

———.1969. *Urban Dynamics*. Cambridge: MIT Press.

———.1973. *World Dynamics. 2nd Edition*. Cambridge: Wright-Allen Press.

Galloway, Alexander. 2004. *Protocol: How Control Exists after Decentralization*. Cambridge: MIT Press.

Hacking, Ian. 1990. *The Taming of Chance*. Cambridge: Cambridge University Press.

———.2006. *The Emergence of Probability: A Philosophical Study of Early Ideas about Probability, Induction and Statistical Inference*. Cambridge: Cambridge University Press.

Halpern, Orit, Robert Mitchell, and Bernard D. Geoghegan. 2017. "The Smartness Mandate: Notes toward a Critique." *Grey Room* 68 (Summer): 106–29. https://doi:10.1162/GREY_a_00221.

Heidegger, Martin. 1977. "Die Zeit des Weltbildes (1938)." In *Gesamtausgabe, Volume 5*, 87–88. Frankfurt: Klostermann.

Helbing, Dirk. 2012. "FuturICT: Participatory Computing for our Complex World." *FuturICT*. Accessed December 12, 2022. https://futurict.inn.ac/.

———.2013a. "Globally Networked Risks and How to Respond." *Nature* 497 (2013): 51–59. https://doi.org/10.1038/nature12047.

———.2013b. "A CERN for the Social Sciences." Filmed May 2013 at CERN, Geneva, Switzerland. Vimeo video, 09:13. https://vimeo.com/67225004.

———.2015. *Thinking Ahead: Essays on Big Data, Digital Revolution, and Participatory Market Society*. Cham: Springer.

Helbing, Dirk, and Stefano Balietti. 2011a. "From Social Data Mining to Forecasting Socio-Economic Crises." *European Physics Journal—Special Topics* 195 (2011): 3–68. https://doi.org/10.1140/epjst/e2011-01401-8.

———.2011b. "From Social Simulation to Integrative System Design." *European Physics Journal—Special Topics* 195 (2011): 69–100. https://doi.org/10.1140/epjst/e2011-01402-7.

Helbing, Dirk, and A. Mazloumian. 2009. "Operation regimes and slower-is-faster effect in the control of traffic intersections." *European Physical Journal B* 70 (2): 257–74. https://doi.org/10.1140/epjb/e2009-00213-5.

Helbing, Dirk, Illés J. Farkas, and Tamás Vicsek. 2000. "Freezing by Heating in a Driven Mesoscopic System." *Physical Review Letters* 84 (6): 1240–43. https://doi.org/10.1103/PhysRevLett.84.1240.

Helbing, Dirk, and Peter Seele. 2017. "Turn War Rooms into Peace Rooms." *Nature* 549 (2017): 458. https://doi.org/10.1038/549458c.

Holland, John H. 1992. *Adaptation in Natural and Artificial Systems: An Introductory Analysis with Applications to Biology, Control, and Artificial Intelligence*. Cambridge: MIT Press.

88   Jacobs, Adam. 2009. "The Pathologies of Big Data." *Communications of the ACM* 52 (8): 36–44. https://doi.org/10.1145/1536616.1536632.

Krajewski, Markus, ed. 2004. *Projektemacher: Zur Produktion von Wissen in der Vorform des Scheiterns*. Berlin: Kadmos.

Lovelock, James E., and Lynn Margulis. 1974. "Atmospheric Homeostasis by and for the Biosphere: The Gaia Hypothesis." *Tellus* 26 (1-2): 2–10. https://doi.org/10.3402/tellusa.v26i1-2.9731.

Luhmann, Niklas. 1994. *Soziale Systeme: Grundriß einer allgemeinen Theorie*. Frankfurt: Suhrkamp.

———.2000. "Die Paradoxie des Entscheidens." In *Organisation und Entscheidung*, 123–51. Wiesbaden: VS Verlag für Sozialwissenschaften.

Mahr, Bernd. 2003. "Modellieren: Beobachtungen und Gedanken zur Geschichte des Modellbegriffs." In *Bild—Schrift—Zahl*, edited by Horst Bredekamp and Sybille Krämer, 59–85. München: Fink.

McLoughlin, J. Brian, and Judith N. Webster. 1970. "Cybernetic and General-System Approaches to Urban and Regional Research: A Review of the Literature." *Environment and Planning* 2 (4): 369–408. https://doi.org/10.1068/a020369.

Meadows, Donella H., Dennis L. Meadows, Jørgen Randers, and William W. Behrens III, eds. 1972. *The Limits to Growth: A Report for the Club of Rome's Project on the Predicament of Mankind*. New York: Universe Books.

Medina, Eden. 2011. *Cybernetic Revolutionaries: Technology and Politics in Allende's Chile*. Cambridge: MIT Press.

Meyers, Robert A., ed. 2009. *Encyclopedia of Complexity and Systems Science*. New York: Springer.

Monchaux, Nicolas de. 2016. *Local Code: 3659 Proposals About Data, Design and the Nature of Cities*. New York: Princeton Architectural Press.

Monge, Fernando, Sarah Barns, Rainer Kattel, and Francesca Bria. 2022. "A New Data Deal: The Case of Barcelona." *UCL Institute for Innovation and Public Purpose, Working Paper Series* 2022 (2): 1–26. https://www.ucl.ac.uk/bartlett/public-purpose/wp2022-02.

Moreno, Carlos. n.d. "Beyond the Smart City." *PCA Stream*. Accessed December 12, 2022. https://www.pca-stream.com/en/articles/carlos-moreno-beyond-the-smart-city-114.

Morgan, Gareth. 2010. "Earth Project Aims to 'Simulate Everything'." *BBC News*, December 28, 2010. http://www.bbc.co.uk/news/technology-12012082.

Morozov, Evgeny. 2013. To Save Everything, Click Here: The Folly of Technological Solutionism. New York: Public Affairs.

Morozov, Evgeny, and Francesca Bria. 2018. *Rethinking the Smart City: Democratizing Urban Technology*. New York: Rosa Luxemburg Stiftung. https://sachsen.rosalux.de/fileadmin/rls_uploads/pdfs/sonst_publikationen/rethinking_the_smart_city.pdf.

O'Sullivan, David, and Mordechai Haklay. 2000. "Agent-Based Models and Individualism: Is the World Agent-Based?" *Environmental Planning A: Economy and Space* 32 (8): 1409–25. https://doi.org/10.1068/a32140.

Pentland, Alex. 2015. *Social Physics: How Social Networks Can Make Us Smarter.* New York: Penguin.

Pias, Claus. 2004. "Zeit der Kybernetik: Eine Einstimmung." In *Cybernetics/Kybernetik: The Macy Conferences. Vol. 2: Documents/Dokumente*, edited by Claus Pias, 9–41. Berlin: Diaphanes.

Pörksen, Bernhard. 2018. *Die große Gereiztheit: Wege aus der kollektiven Erregung.* Munich: Hanser.

Priesemann, Viola, Michael Meyer-Hermann, Iris Pigeot, and Anita Schöbel. 2021. "Der Beitrag von epidemiologischen Modellen zur Beschreibung des Ausbruchsgeschehens der COVID-19-Pandemie." *Bundesgesundheitsblatt* 64 (2021): 1058–66. https://doi.org/10.1007/s00103-021-03390-1.

Ramos, José. 2015. "Liquid Democracy and the Futures of Governance." In *Future Internet: Alternative Visions*, edited by Jenifer Winter and Ryota Ono, 173–91. Cham: Springer.

Reckwitz, Andreas. 2019. *Die Gesellschaft der Singularitäten.* Frankfurt: Suhrkamp.

Rössler, Otto E. 2008. "Interview: Chaos, Verschwörung, schwarze Löcher." By Jens Ihlenfeld. *Golem.de*, February 8, 2008. https://www.golem.de/0802/57477.html.

Rosenberg, Daniel. 2013. "Data Before the Fact." In *"Raw Data" is an Oxymoron*, edited by Lisa Gitelman, 15–40. Cambridge: MIT Press.

Schich, Maximilian, Chaoming Song, Yong-Yeol Ahn, Alexander Mirsky, et al. 2014. "A Network Framework of Cultural History." *Science* 345 (6196): 558–62. https://doi.org/10.1126/science.1240064.

Seefried, Elke. 2015. *Zukünfte. Aufstieg und Krise der Zukunftsforschung 1945–1980.* Oldenbourg: De Gruyter.

Simon, Herbert. 1983. *Reason in Human Affairs.* Stanford: Stanford University Press.

Tabarrok, Alex. 2018. "Will AI become Intelligent enough to figure out how to perfectly organise our economies?" *Quora*, March 1, 2018. https://www.quora.com/Will-AI-become-intelligent-enough-to-figure-out-how-to-perfectly-organise-our-economies/answer/Alex-Tabarrok.

Thurner, Stefan. 2011. "Comments by S. Thurner on the Visioneer white papers by D. Helbing and S. Balietti." *European Physics Journal—Special Topics* 195 (2011): 161–63. https://doi.org/10.1140/epjst/e2011-01409-0.

Thurner, Stefan, Rudolf Hanel, and Peter Klimek. 2018. *Introduction to the Theory of Complex Systems.* Oxford: Oxford University Press.

Waldrop, M. Mitchell. 1992. *Complexity: The Emerging Science at the Edge of Order and Chaos.* New York: Simon & Schuster.

White, Tom. 2009. *Hadoop: The Definitive Guide.* Sebastopol: O'Reilly.

Wiener, Norbert. 1964. *Extrapolation, Interpolation, and Smoothing of Stationary Time Series.* Cambridge: MIT Press.

Wolfram, Stephen. 2002. *A New Kind of Science.* Champaign: Wolfram Media Inc.

Zuboff, Shoshana. 2019. *The Age of Surveillance Capitalism: The Fight for a Human Future at the New Frontier of Power.* New York: Public Affairs.

CYBERNETICS

TELEPRINTER

DATA

NETWORKS

CHILE

4

Encoding from/to the Real: On Cybersyn's Symbolic Politics of Transmission

Diego Gómez-Venegas

This chapter traces the techno-epistemological relevance of Project Cybersyn's processes of production quantification at factories, the transmission of that data, and the road towards their computation. By unfolding a media-archaeological analysis, these pages discuss archival documents showing that from the depths of Project Cybersyn's technologies of transmission and computation, new corre-lations of forces and strategies of organization emerge. In sum, this text provides concrete evidence on how a media archaeology of Project Cybersyn unravels the media-genealogical scope of this case.

A media-archaeological analysis of Project Cybersyn—the tele-communications and processing system developed by Stafford Beer and his team in the early 1970s to manage Chile's economy—can be deployed, these pages argue, under three interconnected commands; namely, *"Encode, Forget,* and *Govern."* This chapter, however, is devoted to the first command only; that is, *"Encode."* Accordingly, a study of the project's modeling of industrial production, of its telecommunications infrastructure, as well as of the configuration and transmission of data, will be developed. The aim of this study is to identify and discuss the *frictions* that may have arisen between the attempts to implement these modeling techniques and the cybernetic thinking supporting them, and on the other hand, *the real* operations at the factories and in the network that they were connected to.

Hence, this chapter will first cover Project Cybersyn's early stages of encoding, in which a group of Chilean engineers visited and modeled the production operations of the factories the project sought to connect. Secondly, the telecommunications infrastructure used for the process of networking will be discussed—here, special attention will be paid to the protocols of encoding, and their potential relation to Chile's early history of telecommunications. Third, a media-theoretical analysis on the previous two aspects will be developed. In the wake of Foucault's archaeological approach, a techno-historical and techno-epistemological problematization will be attempted. Using the notion of *"exchanging"* as a probe, this analysis will traverse the project's operational modeling techniques, its technological infrastructure, and protocols, to finally propose a conceptual device called *tele[economy]cations.*

Prolegomenon

The events discussed in this chapter begin with two pieces of machine-typed paper written in English (fig. 1 and 2). On July 13, 1971, a 28-year-old engineer named Fernando Flores—who Salvador Allende's government had recently appointed as the technical general manager of Chile's Agency of Development (CORFO), as well as the board president of the country's Institute of Technological Research (INTEC)—sent a letter to the cybernetician Stafford Beer. In this letter, Flores not only introduced the British scientist-consultant to the socialist changes happening in Chile's industrial and financial sectors, but also acknowledged the role that his book *Decision and Control* and the operational research methods Beer had developed at the consultancy company SIGMA had played in his own career. More substantially, Flores emphasized the relevance of implementing "scientific views on management and organization" in Chile's socialist process, and how "cybernetic thinking [had become] a necessity" (Flores 1971) for such an implementation. Finally, the Chilean engineer closed his letter asking Beer for advice, as well as for his more recent writings on the topic, and he expressed his hope that Beer could one day visit Chile.

The exchange continued, following quite similar protocols. On July 29, Stafford Beer sent a machine-typed letter in response to Flores, in which—reinforcing the British spelling of Flores's missive, whereby the CORFO engineers Raul Espejo and Juan Bulnes had, in effect, contributed to the writing process in order to secure the proper use of that syntax (Raul Espejo, in discussion with the author, January 29, 2019)—Beer referred to his two upcoming books, *Brain of the Firm* and *Platform for Change*, explaining how they would connect to the problems Chile was facing (Beer 1971a). Asking if Chile's Embassy in London could operate as a proper channel, he added that he would attempt to send Flores a final copy of the former book, and a manuscript of the latter. That is to say, Beer replied with a confirmation

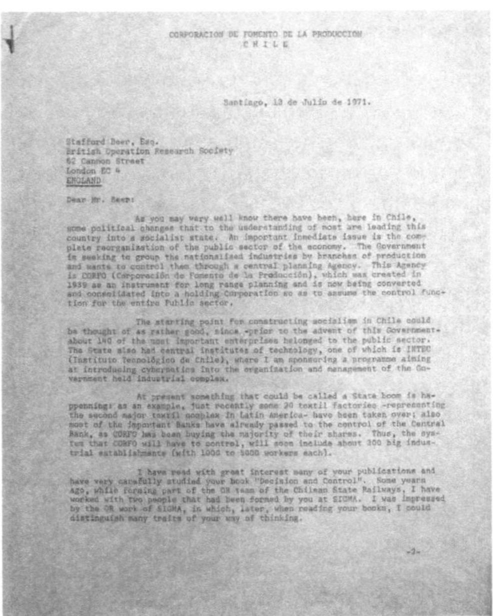

[Fig. 1] Letter from Fernando Flores to Stafford Beer, July 13, 1971. Page 1. (Source: Flores 1971, 1). Courtesy of the Stafford Beer Archive, Liverpool John Moores University, Special Collections & Archives.

message to Flores's request, corroborating the availability of the information sought, while including a request to secure an adequate sending channel. More important, however, was Beer's rhetorical query at the end of the letter. He wondered how he "could [actually] play a part" in this enterprise, since he had "the most extraordinary feelings about this situation" (Beer 1971a).

Beer traveled to Santiago de Chile on November 1, 1971, put together a team, and thus began Project Cybersyn. The plan entailed connecting all the state-owned industrial companies – many of which had been nationalized through methods some considered controversial (Beer [1981] 1994, 246-47)—to collect

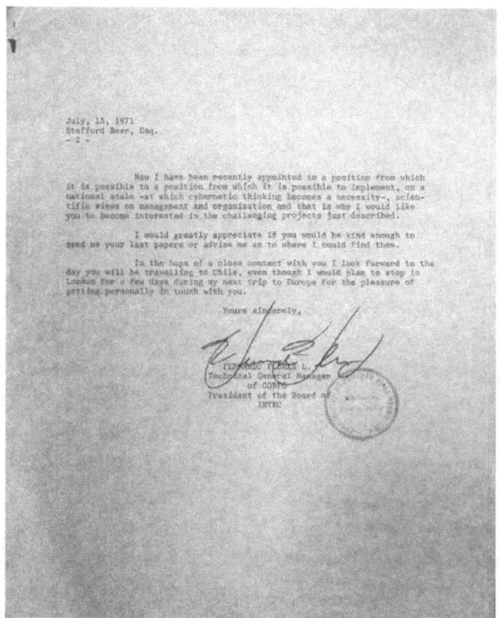

[Fig. 2] Letter from Fernando Flores to Stafford Beer, July 13, 1971. Page 2. (Source: Flores 1971, 2). Courtesy of the Stafford Beer Archive, Liverpool John Moores University, Special Collections & Archives.

daily production data. That data would then be computed in order to obtain its current and potential fluctuations, with the aim to improve the management of the industrial economy both at a local and national scale. This led to the structuring of a plan comprised of four sub-projects: a) a network of telecommunications which would transmit the data, transforming the factories into nodes—this network would later be called *Cybernet*; b) a central computational unit which would receive and analyze the data to forecast behaviors through statistical models – this unit and the software suite it ran would be named *Cyberstride*; c) an additional computational simulation model of the economy which would allow the government to test future scenarios—called *CHECO*, the acronym for Chilean Economy; and finally d) an operations and decisions room, where the processed data would be presented as graphs and diagrams in displays controlled by small keyboard interfaces located at the armrests of seven chairs—the so-called *Opsroom.*

Although Project Cybersyn has largely become known for its *Opsroom*—or, more precisely, because of the appealing images of this room that have circulated throughout the Internet for 15 years or so—this chapter proposes a rather different approach. The reason for that, it is argued here, is that an endeavor aiming to trace the techno-epistemological and cybernetic scope of a project like Cybersyn must first study its *operational core*, and, as it were, only then go up. In other words, an undertaking that emerges from the technologies that made the project's media processes possible; an inquiry that starting with the hardware and software that transmitted, computed, and stored the information the project used, can prompt us to ask about the position, role, and exchanges that humans and machines held in this context. That is, an investigation on the "set of strategies of the relations of forces supporting, and supported by, certain types of knowledge" (Foucault 1980, 196). These pages contend that therein lie the questions that will reveal the true archaeological fibers of Project Cybersyn, and, to anticipate already, its genealogical threads too.

Therefore, this chapter is focused on *Cybernet*—the telecommunications network—and *Cyberstride*—the computational processing unit. Or, paraphrasing Stafford Beer, on the nerves and the brain of a way of governing (Beer 1974, 43). More particularly, the aim here is to tackle the discursive and technological exchanges that configured *Cybernet*—the nerves— by emphasizing the role played by this sub-project's technique of encoding; which will help us trace "the strategies of relations" (Foucault 1980, 196) that in turn set the groundwork for the emergence of a *symbolic* politics of transmission within the overall project.

Protocols

Cybernet's earliest phase required quantitative modeling of the internal operations of the project's factories. This was essential in order to achieve Cybersyn's general goal; that is, "to install a preliminary system of information for the industrial economy that will demonstrate the main features of cybernetic management and begin to help in the task of actual decision making by 1st March 1972" (Beer [1981] 1994, 251–52). Already in his first visit to Santiago, Beer outlined an information system that would be based on data flows, for which the operations at the factories had to be encoded into quantifiable means. For such a task, Beer requested the formation of a team that should include what he then called an "OR Man," and whose professional profile should fit the following description: "Not USA archetype. 'Decision and Control' supporter! Versed in philosophy of science. Biological background ideal" (Beer 1971b, 6). Although these prerequisites were not matched entirely; they were indeed matched in general—a topic for which a small digression is necessary.

The teaching and practice of operational research (OR) was already well established in Chile by the early 1970s. In fact, the first courses in this field began to be taught at schools of engineering around 1957. One of the pioneers of this discipline was Raul Espinosa Wellmann, an engineer and professor at the Catholic University of Chile. After a random discovery at a local bookstore, followed by a more targeted book selection while visiting the USA during the 1950s, Espinosa Wellmann taught himself this discipline, and then introduced the first courses on operational research for students of the Department of Industrial Engineering at the aforementioned university—not much later renamed the Department of Industrial and *Systems* Engineering (Espinosa Wellmann, in discussion with the author, December 2, 2019). Espinosa Wellmann is mentioned by Stafford Beer in one of his early reports from January 1972, where, while discussing the necessity of having a "Chilean Systems Centre" that could act as a supporting institution for the development of Project Cybersyn, and suggesting that this could be achieved by founding a local chapter of the Society of General Systems Research, Beer points out that "to [his] astonishment," he had discovered that such a group already existed, and that it had a regular "programme of meetings in Santiago," which counted Espinosa Wellmann among its members (Beer 1972, 15).

The introduction and development of OR had already influenced Cybersyn's local team, particularly the engineers at CORFO. Many of them had studied at the School of Engineering of the Catholic University of Chile during the 1960s and had been trained in operational research by Espinosa Wellmann and others. Such is the case of Fernando Flores, who, as a young engineer in the OR team at the State Railways Company—years before Cybersyn—worked with the British consultants sent to Chile by Beer's company SIGMA (Flores 1971). Coincidentally, also while traveling in the USA, Flores made a random discovery by which he purchased Beer's book *Decision and Control*, which he later introduced to his peers in Chile (Raul Espejo, in discussion with the author, January 29, 2019). Put differently, these events are connected by a series of information exchanges where university teaching, engineering practices at technical enterprises, as well as random findings at bookstores—as to recall Friedrich Kittler's theories (1981; [1985] 1990; [1986] 1999)—play a significant role.

Coming back to *Cybernet*'s modeling at the factories—which the Cybersyn team used to call "indexes lifting" (Raul Espejo, in discussion with the author, May 19, 2019), somehow suggesting that they would be literally picked up from *"the real"*—it seems important to note how the techniques used for such a process emerged, were implemented, and then were deployed in the context of the project. An initial trace of this can be found in the notes Beer made during his first visit to Santiago. There, in a set of 10 loose pages taken from a sketchbook, one can find a series of quickly-drawn diagrams with comments. In one of them it is possible to read "quantified flowcharts," right next to a drawing with the caption "identify the size of chambers flow ... identify bottlenecks" (Beer 1971c). This technique of *quantified flow-charting* was central to the project's initial stages; first, in regard to the methodological cohesion among the modeling engineers, and second, in the actual fieldwork at the factories. A later document, a thorough report developed by one of the team's engineers, allows us to assess the extent of such a technique.

Officially published by CORFO, signed by Humberto Gabella, and shared with the team in March 1973, the 102-page booklet titled *A Quantified Flowcharting Technique for Real-Time Control* constituted a detailed methodological tool for modeling production activity at the factories. Accordingly, the report stated that its goal was to support the implementation of "management techniques that have been developed ... to be transformed into effective governing tools at the service of all levels of decision within the industrial apparatus" (Gabella 1973, 1).[1] After an introduction to general flowcharting—which defined key concepts, explained its arithmetic, and gave examples of companies already modeled by the team—it followed an account of the scope of the notion of quantification in the context of this technique. By acknowledging that flowcharting consisted of detecting the flows that connect the "elements" that dynamically form "any productive system," and considering that "for the implementation of this technique [such elements] must be considered 'black-boxes'" (Gabella 1973, 2), the use of quantification entailed, first, to detect the variables conditioning the flows, to then measure the ratio between their *real* level at a given time, and their *actual* capacity. Such a ratio was then graphically expressed in a diagram in order to effec-tively communicate the intensity of that index.

Three questions must be considered at this point. First, by under-standing all productive "elements" of a system as black boxes, the technique embraced two key notions from Beer's management cybernetics: *recursion* and *variety* (fig. 3). The former notion

---

1   Document retrieved from Raul Espejo's personal archive.

implies that the elements of a system are closed sub-systems containing other closed sub-systems, and that each of these contain others—and so on. It follows that every sub-system in the recursion must be supervised, and internally known, only by the team in charge of that sub-system—all sub-systems and teams are thus ruled by a general principle of autonomy. Consequently, the technique allows those in charge of the general system, as well as those in charge of sub-systems, to pay attention to the interactions between the elements within the supervised sub-system only—what happens in neighboring sub-systems is, as it were, another team's business. Therefore, from the point of view of Beer's management cybernetics, this constituted an initial step towards the filtering of *variety*—i.e., the complexity of the system—and increasing autonomy, thus assuring the viability of that system. Second, the quantitative modeling of the relations between *flows* and *elements* would allow the detection of *bottlenecks* in the system, to thus select the key, conditioning variables of the workflow. This is particularly relevant because Project Cybersyn, as a whole, operated by modeling a wide range of variables, while however only processing a sample of them—which marks a key difference with contemporary data processing. Third, in the background of these considerations, on one hand Beer had already argued, in *Decision and Control*, that the collection and parsing of too many variables in the process of modeling a company was an actual problem for the manager aiming to control a productive system (Beer [1966] 1994, 96–98), and that therefore management cybernetics should provide ways to attenuate such a *variety* (Beer [1966] 1994, 289–98). On the other hand, however, an even more concrete matter emerged when the Cybersyn team faced *the real* fact that they had very limited access to infrastructure, equipment, and computational capacity to implement the project. Therefore, in contrast to the scientific ideal that demanded that the manager analyze the whole scope of variables detected in a system (Beer [1966] 1994, 97), Beer and his team had to rely on this quantified flowcharting technique and the nuances it proposed.

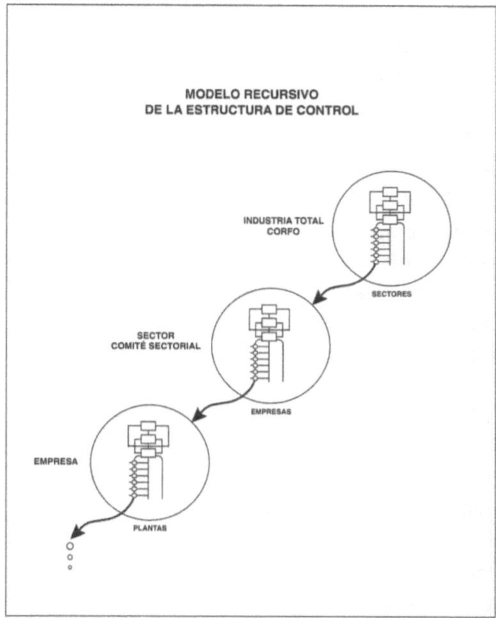

[Fig. 3] Stafford Beer's notion of recursion applied to his Viable System Model. Redrawn by the author from Raul Espejo's report "Proyecto Synco: Conceptos y práctica del control" (Source: Espejo 1973, 14).

This implied that the modeling of the factories would almost be a tailor-made process, where each case would go through a particular process of analysis, and thus through a specific quantified flowcharting. In other words, the OR team recognized that each factory was a system or rather a sub-system in its own right, even if it was part of an industrial branch—e.g., the timber industry—and that it would then have a particular set of variables. This time-consuming process was by no means an automated one—it was always developed by OR men. Only equipped with their training in operational research and the aforementioned technique, these men visited the factories and studied their operations. In a way—and this was part of the "noise" the Cybersyn team had to accept—this process included a fair degree of subjectivity (Beer [1966] 1994, 99). Let's consider for example the case of the textile industrial branch, which was then an important part of Chile's industrial economy. The modeling of such a branch was the responsibility of Tomás Kohn; a 28-year-old engineer who had studied at a technical university in the Chilean city of Valparaiso. It was there that Kohn first became acquainted with operational research, in his case through programming. Kohn attended Fortran courses taught by Wolfgang Riesenkönig—a German programmer who had moved to Chile to install the first Lorenz ER-56 digital computer in 1962 (Álvarez and Gutiérrez 2012a, 5). Later, supported by a Fulbright scholarship, Kohn studied in the USA, receiving his master's degree from Louisiana State University, where he delved into OR, statistics, and automatic control. As Kohn recalls, the process of modeling involved visiting the factories, and using the technique of quantified flowcharting, as well as several long meetings at INTEC to discuss the theoretical aspects that would help the team to better interpret Beer's work, the technique in question, and its results—a process certainly driven by technical skills, but, as Kohn states, also arrogance (Tomás Kohn, in discussion with the author, December 9, 2019).

An additional distinction becomes necessary here. It has been claimed, particularly by the US historian of informatics Eden Medina (2011, 101), but also by Beer himself in later interviews and writings (Beer 1974, 47)—perhaps as an attempt to match Cybersyn's politics of technology to Allende's socialist program—that factory workers had participated in, or that the project's original design considered them taking part in, Cybersyn's processes of modeling and the subsequent decision-making. However, concerning the modeling of production and its indexes, the findings of the research behind these pages suggest something different. When it comes to Cybersyn's politics of transmission—that is, the exchange of scientific discourses, techniques, technologies, data, and information—it seems clearer every day that what took place at *Cybernet* is interwoven with the old protocols of university teaching, academic papers, scientific and technical treatises, and operational reports—and whose carriers were, after all and mostly (although *not always*), highly skilled engineers.

Infrastructure

Nonetheless, new protocols were also part of *Cybernet*; they came from the fields of telecommunications and computing, and their configuration was determined to a great extent by the infrastructure and equipment available in the country. Beer was well aware, years before Cybersyn, of the role that computation should play in operational research, and, all the more, in the development of management cybernetics—because, as he stated in 1966, "this [was] the age of 'automatic data processing'" (Beer [1966] 1994, 70). For Beer, the main goal of his cybernetic approach to management and control was, literally, a matter of time:

> Even the most advanced countries in the world suffer from a vast lag in the receipt of economic data, and they suffer too from the bureaucratic time it takes to process these data towards any kind of conclusion. (Beer [1981] 1994, 248)

Beer argued that developed nations still had a lack of awareness regarding what "the current state of telecommunications and the computing art" (Beer [1981] 1994, 248) was, and what it could do to reduce the time of analysis of economic data, whose results used to arrive with an "average delay of nine months" (Beer [1981] 1994, 248). Therefore, he insisted that moving towards real-time processing was the only way to reach an effective level of data analysis, and thus of economic management. However, Beer and his team in Chile faced a difficult scenario, where the available technology was, in the cybernetician's own words, "antiquated" (Beer [1981] 1994, 248). Additionally, the chances to invest in new equipment were almost zero, in large part due to the political constraints affecting Allende's government regarding the international exchange of goods. Thus, despite the fact that the ideal design required interconnecting all the factories taking part in the project through a distributed network of *teleprocessing*—where each plant would have an in-house computer to process all the data that were "vital" for its operations (Beer [1981] 1994, 252)—*the real* circumstances demanded something different. By 1971, Chile had only 57 computers; most of them being mainframes heavily used by either universities or administrative institutions (Álvarez and Gutiérrez 2012b, 28; Medina 2011, 60). On the other hand, being that Chile was then a poor country under strong political and economic pressure, buying new machines was not a viable option—consider here that the project aimed to connect over 100 companies, and that the price of a mainframe computer ranged between US$1 and US$2 million (Álvarez and Gutiérrez 2014, 131–35). Therefore, the team was forced—knowing that the project still required a reliance on the old Greek *tèle* (τῆλε)—to replace the word *processing* with the powers of transmission granted by *communications*. Thus, they looked at a reliable technology that by the 1970s had a robust infrastructure in the country; namely, *telex* networks.

Nonetheless, an important distinction has to be made here. One that acknowledges a key aspect of Eden Medina's unpublished PhD thesis (2005), and which—even if she decided not to emphasize it in *Cybernetic Revolutionaries*—is fundamental to assessing the scope of what follows. Despite the antiquatedness of Chile's technology as pointed out by Beer, the country had, not long before Cybersyn began, gone through what can be understood as a major technological transformation. In the government that preceded Allende's—the one led by the Christian Democrat, Eduardo Frei Montalva from 1964 to 1970—key developments unfolded: in 1964, the National Enterprise of Telecommunications (ENTEL) was put together, seeking to enhance and control the development of telecommunications in the country; in 1967, the National Commission on Computation was created with the

specific goal of advising the government on the use of computing;
in 1968, a National Enterprise of Computation (EMCO, later ECOM) was founded by and within the government, aiming to provide computing services to all the divisions of the state; and then, the same year, the aforementioned Institute of Technological Research (INTEC) was established. All these, alongside other efforts in the same direction, were benefited by, and in some way possible thanks to, foreign financial aid such as that coming from the USA's Alliance for Progress program (Medina 2005, 108–65; Álvarez 2014, 18–26).

Accordingly, ECOM acquired first an IBM 360/40 mainframe computer, and in 1970 another of this model as well as an IBM 360/50 (Álvarez 2014, 26)—machines that had been released on the market in August 1965, and were sold by IBM until 1977 (IBM n.d.). On the other hand, ENTEL inherited the technical management of part of a telex network inaugurated in 1959, but which had been heavily extended and technologically updated in 1967—a network originally developed by Chile's State Post and Telegraph Company on top of its own, old telegraph network (Diehl 1970, 21–37). This network's main station was in Santiago, with major line connections to the city of Valparaiso on the central Pacific coast, Concepcion in the south, and La Serena in the north (fig. 4). From the latter two, connections to smaller cities were established, and from Santiago, radio HF links activated nodes in the further north and south of the country (Diehl 1970, 35)—consider here that Chile is over 4,000 kilometers long, and that the far north and south offer particularly rugged geographical conditions. Moreover, the network also included a station of satellite links for international communications, which, 100 kilometers away from Santiago, was inaugurated in 1968 as the first of its kind on the continent (ENTEL-Chile ca. 1971).

Regarding the equipment used by this network, in 1965 the government granted concessions to two foreign companies as part of an expansion plan. Consequently, the machinery and technical support to build and maintain the central routing

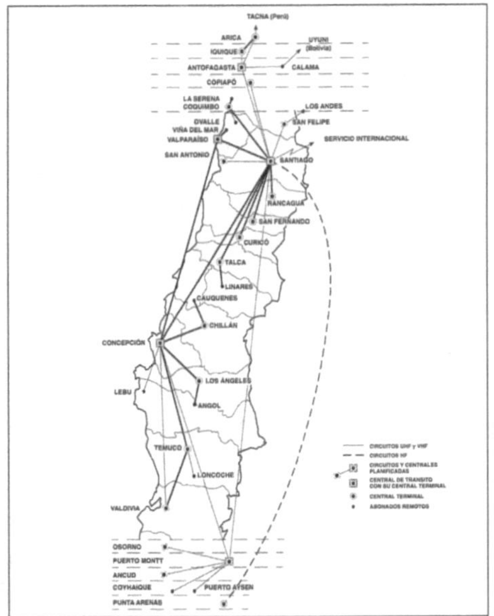

[Fig. 4] Telex Network in Chile by 1970. Redrawn by the author from Lothar Diehl's *La Telegrafía en Chile*. (Source: Diehl 1970, 35).

stations was provided by Sweden's LM Ericsson (Diehl 1970, 27), which installed switching systems of the type ARB-111 and ARM-201 in the country (Ruiz Zúñiga 1976, 9–11).

Concerning smaller equipment, a brief digression is necessary. Medina and others have claimed that while working on the telex network, and facing a lack of machinery to complete this work, Project Cybersyn's team was fortunate enough to find hundreds of unused teleprinters in an ENTEL storage facility (Medina 2011, 72; Becket 2003). These claims, which have no formal reference, do not provide many details about the finding, nor about the type of equipment it consisted of. Hence, although the facts surrounding that discovery are still a missing link for the research sustaining these pages, it is now possible to offer some clarifications. When, in 1965, Chile's Ministry of Interior granted

[Fig. 5] The Siemens T-100 Teleprinter. Views from Service Manual. (Source: Siemens & Halske Aktiengesellschaft 1963, VI.3). Courtesy of Siemens Historical Institute.

the concession to provide teleprinting and harmonic telegraphy equipment for the country's public telex network, the recipient was the German company Siemens (Diehl 1970, 27). Moreover, when it comes to teleprinters in particular, the model acquired by Chile was the T-100 (fig. 5), and it is possible to state here that by April 1973 ENTEL had 265 units—215 in use, and 50 in stock—while the State Post and Telegraph Company had 1,063, of which only 182 were in stock (CORFO 1973, 43). Therefore, if the discovery of the unused teleprinters did indeed take place, this would have referred to a storage facility of the latter company. More simply, it was never about 400 or 500 units, but a rather smaller amount—consider again that Project Cybersyn aimed to connect some 100 factories (Medina 2011, 86).

In a word, it was under these circumstances that the Cybersyn team would have found the equipment, and thus arranged and configured *Cybernet*. It is also true that some private telecommunications companies with a presence in Chile, such as the International Telephone & Telegraph Company (ITT)—secret exchanges with the CIA notwithstanding (Secretaría General de Gobierno 1972; Committee on Foreign Relations United States Senate 1973)—could have used British Creed teleprinters, and it is also possible that local armed forces used the American Teletype Corporation Model 33 ASR for their own closed telex networks (Ministerio de Defensa de Chile 1974). Nonetheless, as the widespread use in the public sector shows—e.g., the State Railways Company, which had its own network too (Orlando Contreras, in discussion with the author, December 19, 2019)—the Siemens T-100 teleprinter was by far the standard in the country.

Furthermore, the telex network used by the Cybersyn team had an identification system for subscribers—i.e., connected teleprinters—consisting of a five-digit code. The first two digits represented the area where the subscriber was located: the first indicated the region—Chile's central region was number 4—and the second referred to a district within that region—Santiago had the number 0. Thus, when subscribers in a southern region wanted to connect with a subscriber in the district of Santiago, they began by dialing 4 and 0. The remaining three digits identified the actual subscriber (Diehl 1970, 32–34). Given the increasing direct exchanges between national and international subscribers, the Chilean authorities introduced a protocol which, following the recommendations of the UN's International Telegraph and Telephone Consultative Committee (CCITT), gave each telex node an international identifier formed by a series of 20 signals that every teleprinter sent at the beginning of a message (Diehl 1970, 34). The series was structured as follows:

Signal: 1 2 3 4 5 6 7 8 9 10 11 12 13 14 15 16 17 18 19 20
Combination: ↓ < = ↑ N N N N N → ↓ X X X X X → C L ↓

Where,

↓	Shift to letter
↑	Shift to numbers
→	Space
<	Carriage return
=	Enter (line break)
NNNNN	National number
XXXXX	Subscriber information
CL	Chile's ID

The structure above can be seen in a telex message found at the Stafford Beer Archive in Liverpool (fig. 6). Starting with the header, it is possible to notice: first, a shift to letters (↓); and then a line break (<). In order to make a small code analysis, let's jump to the fourth line, skipping the two red lines in the middle. The message shifts then to numbers (↑), presenting a five-digit figure (NNNNN) where the first two are 4 and 0—i.e., the subscriber was from the Santiago district. There follows a space (→) and a shift to letters again (↓); it reads CORFO—the Chilean development agency. After that, there is another space (→) and the CL code. It perfectly matches the protocol shown above.

Regarding the first two letters of this telex—G and A—further research has yet to be completed. However, the mere fact that the code begins with letters tells us something interesting. According to a report found at the documentation center of the Chilean Ministry of Transport and Telecommunications—the one informing these paragraphs—"the machines used in Chile (Siemens T 100)" had a default feature that made them begin every exchange with a shift to letter signal (Diehl 1970, 34). On the other hand, the color coding in the text was designed to identify between outgoing messages, in red, and incoming ones, in black (Siemens & Halske Aktiengesellschaft 1963, V.3). Consequently, it is possible to notice that the message from the Stafford Beer Archive was in fact printed at ECOM, and that the black text was incoming data from the receiver subscriber; in this case, a teleprinter at CORFO—with both sender and receiver located in Santiago.

Another relevant aspect can be found in the footer of this message (fig. 7). The small cross indicates the "who are you" symbol, which gave information regarding the identities of the parties involved in an exchange. More interestingly, not all teleprinters printed that square, Prussian-style cross as the Siemens T-100 did (Siemens & Halske Aktiengesellschaft 1963, II.9–13)—models from other manufacturers printed either narrower, or thinner and color-filled crosses. In other words, it is possible to confirm

```
GA
40750
40506 ECOM CL
40750 CORFO CL

DE:ECOM.
A :SR.ROBERTO CAÑETE-SALA DE OPERACIONES.

SE HAN DETECTADO LOS SIGUIENTES INFORMES ALGEDONICOS A NIVEL CORFO:
DEL 3-4-73 AL 6-4-73:

INFORMES ENVIADOS A LAS DIFERENTES EMPRESAS Y COMITES .

C/C A DON RAUL ESPEJO.

DE:ECOM.
A :SR.SECRETARIO EJECUTIVO COMITE TEXTIL.
```

[Fig. 6] Telex Message between ECOM and CORFO, April 1973—Header. Stafford Beer Archive, Box 64. Courtesy of the Stafford Beer Archive, Liverpool John Moores University, Special Collections & Archives.

```
RECIBIO CONF??? +++

MENSAJE ENVIADO A LAS 12.30 HRS.
40750 CORFO CL
40506 ECOM CL
```

[Fig. 7] Telex Message between ECOM and CORFO, April 1973—Footer. Stafford Beer Archive, Box 64. Courtesy of the Stafford Beer Archive, Liverpool John Moores University, Special Collections & Archives.

that subscriber number 40506 from Chile's ECOM was a Siemens teleprinter.

Yet, it must be noted that *Cybernet* was configured to support a very specific goal: "To install a preliminary system of information and regulation for the industrial economy" (Beer [1981] 1994, 251). Put differently, beyond the technical specifications of the network and its equipment, the data sent from the factories to the processing center should also have their own protocols. Hence, given that the incoming data had to match the requirements of the software suite being developed by the *Cyberstride* team, these protocols were designed in the offices of ECOM—where the local *Cyberstride* team was based. This was done while paying special attention to the indexes the OR team obtained from the modeling process at the factories. Accordingly, the protocol consisted of a series of codes for each factory, which referred precisely to such indexes (Benadof 1972, 1–5).

For the textile industrial sector for example, a code looked like this: TEXSAIMPEXISTENPOLSTW (Benadof 1972, 2). The codes were formed by 22 letters, where the first three referred to the sector, and the following five indicated the name of the factory. After that, the next 12 letters showed the specific index, in this case "existence polyester," or the stock level of polyester. Similarly, ECOM had prepared a small form which the people at the factories had to fill in with the respective data (Benadof 1972, 2–3). Nonetheless, one question remains: who was seated in front of the teleprinter at the factories and typed out this data? Although the findings of this research on this matter are still not fully conclusive, some preliminary informed conjectures can be offered. Considering that the companies connected to the project used to have departments of industrial operations led by engineers trained in OR—that is the case, for example, for a textile company this research has investigated (Manuel Núñez, in discussion with the author, December 5, 2019)—it is probable that the values of the daily indexes had been collected by members of these departments. Moreover, because those unassuming forms were still simple sheets of paper with blank boxes where letters should be entered, it is also possible that they had been filled out with that old and traditional tool called the pen, before being— as if Kittler's theories were again pushing for the conclusion of this section (Kittler [1986] 1999, 183–263)—transcribed, finally in real contact with the machine, by female secretaries (Isaquino Benadof, in discussion with the author, December 4, 2019; Manuel Núñez, in discussion with the author, December 5, 2019).

> And since power after the print monopoly's collapse was
> diverted to cable and radio, to the recording of traces and

electrical engineering, outdated security protocols were dropped as well (Kittler [1986] 1999, 195).

Tele[economy]cations

Almost 100 years before Cybersyn, in January 1874, another exchange between the Chilean government and a British technology businessman took place (West Coast of America Telegraph Company Limited 1875, 10–11). Strictly ruled by the ceremoniously handwritten protocols of notaries, and of the UK's and Chile's 19th-century legislation (Horacio de Pinna 1898), this triggered a series of commercial transactions and concessions that eventually led to the laying of a submarine cable connecting the Peruvian seaport of El Callao, and its Chilean equivalents in Caldera and Coquimbo at that country's north, and in Valparaiso in the center (West Coast of America Telegraph Company Limited 1875, 10–12). Moreover, these developments brought about the arrival of the British West Coast of America Telegraph Company Limited in Chile, with the subsequent construction of a tele-communications network that—linked to the network built by Clark's Transandine Telegraph Company—connected the main ports and business centers of Chile with Europe, using cable technology that spanned Buenos Aires and Pernambuco, all before 1876 (Diehl 1970, 15–16). The reasons behind such a level of technological entrepreneurship in this remote corner of the world would be hard to explain in detail here. However, it is possible to state that they are strongly linked to the vast deposits of natural resources in the area—e.g., nitrates and copper in the north, as well as coal in the south—and the local governments' great interest in exploiting those resources with the help of foreign capital (Monteón 2003). In a word, the early arrival of telegraphy technology and infrastructure to Chile is inextricably attached to economic exchanges. Its purpose, consequently, was to serve as a platform of communication, supporting commercial transactions and the capital interests behind them.

Therefore, a media-archaeological analysis of Project Cybersyn, and particularly of *Cybernet* and *Cyberstride*, cannot avoid a genealogical approach. If a problematization of Project Cybersyn as an apparatus, as a *dispositif*, is in effect possible, one is compelled to study, as pointed out earlier, the "set of strategies of the relations of forces supporting, and supported by, certain types of knowledge" (Foucault 1980, 196). Accordingly, when a secretary seated in front of a Siemens teleprinter types almost incomprehensible codes, followed by dates and decimal numbers with the goal of transmitting pure economic data, what emerges is *the symbolic* displacement of the centrality of human understanding: a techno-episteme which is invariably attached to a still ungraspable politic of transmission. Its genealogy, however, is undetachable from a longer history of scientific discourses, infrastructure, technology, and information exchanges. One is thus compelled to ask: whose agency would have emerged, then, in Chile's 1970s factories? All the more, is there a component of that agency that could account for the 100-year genealogical transformation in that corner of the world?

An attempt to answer such an inquiry leads to the question of value; its formation, and the place and time where all that is hosted. Then, with the archaeologist, it may be said:

> It is thus no longer a question of knowing in accordance with what mechanism kinds of wealth can represent each other (and represent themselves by means of that universally representative wealth constituted by precious metal), but why objects of desire and need have to be represented, how one posits the value of a thing, and why one can affirm that it is worth this or that (Foucault 2005, 206).

Yet, in that distant and lonely room where the secretary types, who is *the one* that posits the value of a thing, when all that she has at her disposal is a frenetic clacking machine, its keyboard, and a series of puzzling codes? Literally, then, there seems to be *no one*. She fades away *in* the machine, and thus the possibility of

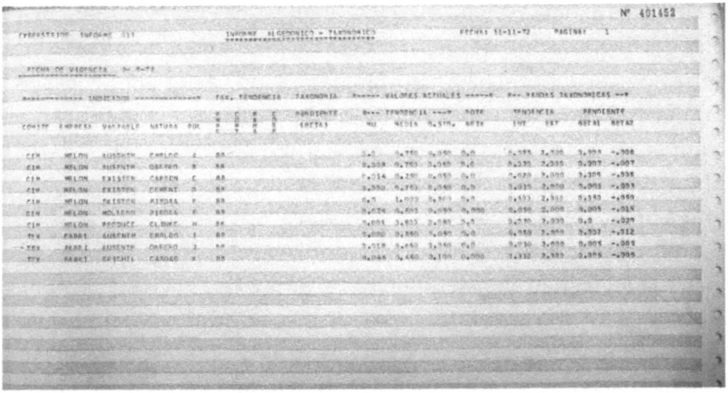

[Fig. 8] Printout of *Cyberstride*'s Permanent Suite. (Source: ECOM 1972, 3). Courtesy of the Stafford Beer Archive, Liverpool John Moores University, Special Collections & Archives.

finding *a single place* for the formation of value is left adrift. This is so because, starting from the teleprinters, throughout the telex network, to the processing center, every place has been replaced by sequences of symbols, and all formations by their constant erasability. Hence, that which this sort of archaeology can no longer tell us could then be pointed out by cybernetic thinking: "That is to say that cybernetics studies the flow of information round a system, and the way in which that information [data, in this case] is used by the system as a means of controlling itself" (Beer [1966] 1994, 254). Put differently, data for the system, and a system for that data. Does this interrelation indicate the moments and the processes through which a new sort of value began to be encoded? One that emerges from feedback, or self-regulation?

Again, if one is able to study Project Cybersyn as a *dispositif*, it must be considered, with Agamben, that starting from Foucault's *positivity* we can traverse the broad and complex notion of *dispositif*, to arrive to the old Greek term *oikonomia*: "the administration of the *oikos* (the home) and, more generally, management" (Agamben 2009, 8). Therefore, could we then problematize Project Cybersyn as an economic system of transmission, processing, and storage of data, and of its encoded value? A system whose ultimate aim is making *its own economic condition* viable? Would this signal a knot shaped by the archaeological and genealogical echoes of a stubborn cybernetic thinking? A knot that could help us unravel the way in which this technological project of management, this technological economy of *dispositions*, thus constitutes a project for governing the *oikos* too?

The notion of *tele[economy]cations* aims to highlight these questions; to emphasize the ways in which they could activate an analysis and a discussion on the techniques, technologies, and scientific discourses that interconnect *Cybernet* and *Cyberstride*. This sort of approach requires, nonetheless, a materially grounded research strategy; one that can prove—against the claims suggesting that Project Cybersyn simply could not have worked—that after all, it did function. That the evidence confirms that, at least in the case of *Cybernet* and *Cyberstride*, they were indeed in operation (fig. 8), and that their features were applied to encode, transmit, and process data from about 20 factories (Isaquino Benadof, in discussion with the author, December 4, 2019) before, 50 years ago, on September 11, 1973, a coup d'état destroyed everything.

The field and archival work behind this chapter was partially funded by Chile's National Agency of Research and Development through the doctoral grant no. 72200037.

References

Agamben, Giorgio. 2009. *"What Is an Apparatus?" and Other Essays*, translated by David Kishik and Stefan Pedatella. Stanford: Stanford University Press.

Álvarez, Juan. 2014. "Empresa Nacional de Computación: Antecedentes, Creación y Primeros Años." *Bits de Ciencia* 10 (1): 18–27.

Álvarez, Juan, and Claudio Gutiérrez. 2012a. "El primer computador universitario en Chile: 'El hogar desde donde salió y se repartió la luz'." *Bits de Ciencia* 8 (1): 2–13.

116 ———.2012b. "History of Computing in Chile, 1961–1982: Early Years, Consolidation, and Expansion." *IEEE Annals of the History of Computing* 34 (3): 22–33.

———.2014. "Empresa Nacional de Computación, Chile: Antecedentes, creación y primeros años." In *Proceedings of the XL Latin American Computing Conference*, edited by Pablo Ezzatti and Andrea Delgado, 128–36. Montevideo: Universidad de la República.

Beckett, Andy. 2003. "Santiago Dreaming." *The Guardian*, September 8, 2003. https://www.theguardian.com/technology/2003/sep/08/sciencenews.chile.

Beer, Stafford. 1971a. Stafford Beer to Fernando Flores, July 29, 1971. Liverpool John Moores University, Stafford Beer Archive, Box 55.

———.1971b. "Project Cyberstride," Santiago, November 1971. Liverpool John Moores University, Stafford Beer Archive, Box 57.

———.1971c. Notes and Sketches from November 1971. Liverpool John Moores University, Stafford Beer Archive, Box 57.

———.1974. *Designing Freedom*. London: John Wiley & Sons.

———.1972. "Cyberstride: Preparations," January 1972. Liverpool John Moores University, Stafford Beer Archive, Box 57.

———.(1981) 1994. *Brain of the Firm, 2nd Edition*. Chichester: John Wiley & Sons.

———.(1966) 1994. *Decision and Control. The Meaning of Operational Research and Management Cybernetics*. Chichester: John Wiley & Sons.

Benadof, Isaquino. 1972. Empresa Nacional de Computación e Informática, Gerencia de Ingeniería, Departamento de Análisis de Sistemas, Manual de Perforación TS - 07, Sistema Cyberstride, Temporary Suite. Liverpool John Moores University, Stafford Beer Archive, Box 57.

Committee on Foreign Relations United States Senate, Subcommittee on Multinational Corporations. 1973. *The International Telephone and Telegraph Company and Chile, 1970–1971*. Washington DC: Congress of the United States of America.

Contreras, Orlando. 2019. (Former technician, Department of Signals, Chile's State Railway Company), in discussion with the author, December.

CORFO. 1973. *Armaduría de Teleimpresores ELECNA*. CORFO, Subgerencia de Industrial Liviana, Comité de Industrial Eléctricas y Electrónicas. Santiago: CORFO.

Diehl, Lothar. 1970. *La Telegrafía en Chile*. Santiago: Dirección Nacional de Correos y Telégrafos, Subdirección de Telecomunicaciones.

ECOM. 1972. Informe Algedónico - Taxonómico, Permanent Suite. Liverpool John Moores University, Stafford Beer Archive, Box 57.

ENTEL-Chile. ca. 1971. Promotional flyer, "National Telecommunications Company—ENTEL-Chile." Liverpool John Moores University, Stafford Beer Archive, Box 64.

Espejo, Raul. 1973. *Proyecto Synco: Conceptos y práctica del control, una experiencia concreta: La dirección industrial de Chile*. Santiago: CORFO

———.2019. (Former director of operations, Project Cybersyn, CORFO), in discussion with the author. January.

———.2019. (Former director of operations, project Cybersyn, CORFO), in discussion with the author. May.

Espinosa Wellmann, Raul. 2019. (Former systems engineering professor, Pontifical Catholic University of Chile), in discussion with the author. December.

Flores, Fernando. 1971. Fernando Flores to Stafford Beer, July 13, 1971. Liverpool John Moores University, Stafford Beer Archive, Box 55.

Foucault, Michel. 1980. "The Confession of the Flash." In *Power/Knowledge: Selected Interviews and Other Writings, 1972–1977*, edited by Colin Gordon, 194–228. New York: Pantheon Books.

———.2005. *The Order of Things. An Archaeology of the Human Sciences*. London: Routledge Classics.

Gabella, Humberto. 1973. *Técnica de la flujogramación cuantificada para efectos del control en tiempo real. Primera versión*. CORFO. Santiago: CORFO.

Horacio de Pinna. 1898. Contract Under Notary Public for the Laying of Submarine Cable Infrastructure. Chile's Archivo Nacional Historico, Fondo Varios, Folder 1447.

IBM. n.d. "System/360: Dates and characteristics." *IBM*. Accessed January 30, 2020. https://www.ibm.com/ibm/history/exhibits/mainframe/mainframe_FS360.html.

Kittler, Friedrich. 1981. "Forgetting." *Discourse* 3 (Spring): 88–121. https://www.jstor.org/stable/41371590.

———.(1985) 1990. *Discourse Networks, 1800/1900*. Stanford: Stanford University Press.

———.(1986) 1999. *Gramophone, Film, Typewriter*. Stanford: Stanford University Press.

Kohn, Tomás. 2019. (Former operational research engineer, INTEC/CORFO), in discussion with the author. December.

Medina, Eden. 2011. *Cybernetic Revolutionaries: Technology and Politics in Allende's Chile*. Cambridge: MIT Press.

———(as Jessica Eden Miller Medina). 2005. "The State Machine: Politics, Ideology, and Computation in Chile, 1964–1973." PhD diss., MIT.

Ministerio de Defensa de Chile. 1974. "Aprueba nuevo reglamento de tasas y derechos aeronáuticos y deroga el decreto supremo (AV.) 90, de 19 de Febrero de 1969," Decree 124, Santiago de Chile. https://www.leychile.cl/N?i=273268&f=1974-04-10&p=.

Monteón, Michael. 2003. "John T. North, the Nitrate King, and Chile's Lost Future." *Latin American Perspectives* 30 (6): 69–90. https://www.jstor.org/stable/3185084.

Núñez, Manuel. 2019. (Former textile worker, Yarur Textile Company), in discussion with the author. December.

Ruiz Zúñiga, Manuel H. 1976. "Enlace Telex." Internship Report, University of Chile.

Secretaría General de Gobierno. 1972. *Los Documentos Secretos de la ITT y la República de Chile: Fotocopias de los Documentos Originales y Traducción Completa del Inglés*. Santiago: Gobierno de Chile.

Siemens & Halske Aktiengesellschaft. 1963. *Siemens Teleprinter 100 Service Manual, June 1963*. Munich: Siemens & Halske Aktiengesellschaft.

West Coast of America Telegraph Company Limited. 1875. Translation of the Peruvian and Chilian Concessions, or Liberties to Land, Maintain, and Work Telegraph Lines, and of the Agreement with the Lima Railway Company. London: Causton & Sons. Chile's Archivo Nacional Historico, Fondo Varios, Folder 1447.

CYBERNETICS

TECHNOLÓGOS

MATTER

DIAGRAMS

5

On the Notion of Cybernetic Frictions and its Role in Radical Media Archaeology

Wolfgang Ernst

This chapter asks to what extent the technical realizations of cybernetic projects still relate to their conceptual diagrams. This is assessed by discussing three types of endeavors: a) those from the early years of cybernetics showing asynchronous frictions between the unfolding of cybernetic thinking and the pace of technological deployment; b) the mid-century attempts to implement cybernetic models in culture and society, where infrastructure itself appears as the source of resistance; and c) the still recurrent efforts to develop diagrammatic and techno-material methods to study the feedback loops between the environ-ment, natural resources, and their industrial

appropriation. Hence, it will be argued that the techno-logical frictions emerging from mate(real)izing cybernetic systems should not be seen simply as collateral damage, nor as noisy disturbances, but rather as an essential component of the techno*lógos* of cybernetics.

This book, as well as the *Applied Cybernetics* lecture series co-organized by the Institute of Musicology and Media Studies at the Humboldt University of Berlin and the Institute of History and Philosophy of Science, Technology, and Literature at the Technical University of Berlin,[1] have not simply been an administrative matter of academic cooperation, but, almost by necessity, a programmatic act. It takes the combined effort of technical analysis—e.g., computer and engineering sciences—and fields in the humanities—e.g., media epistemology, media archaeology, techno-poietics, machine-oriented ontology—to address the temporal moments, and spatial sites where cybernetics as a conceptual frame—the symbolic order—confronts its material *real*—its literal mater(e)alization.

The core drama enacted on the landscape of the technological world stems from the entanglements of logical reasoning with the material real—the *mateReal* in a more Lacanian sense (Kittler 1999). Analog and digital technologies oscillate between *logified* matter and mechanized mind. Thus, *radical* media archaeology becomes an adequate method to investigate concrete scenarios *in*, and *as* the cybernetic media theater. The encounters of technical reason (*lógos*) with in-formable matter occur in two ways: one being method, the other actual realizations. Media science, with media archaeology as its method, radically *grounds* the investigation of technical objects in actual matter, aiming to discover its main sources of action (*archai*). How close can

1   Both conceptually shaped and organized by Diego Gómez-Venegas.

such analytic *lógos* get to what is unfolded within the technical *mateReal*?

According to the research hypothesis of radical media archaeology, it is in these frictions that the techno*lógos* of cybernetic thinking can be found. A *frictionless* functioning of technology-b(i)ased communication, or a "friction-free world" (Tapscott and Tapscott 2016, 265), is a fallacy which does not account for the *veto* of its material implementation. Friction is a term well known from mechanical physics, one that Carl von Clausewitz applied to his seminal theory of war to describe the differences—*Friktionen*—between the strategic diagram and the actual hindrances occurring in its practical implementation (von Clausewitz 1832). In the case of Chile's Project Cybersyn, there were two types of diagrams: the cybernetic design—Stafford Beer's Viable System Model—and the actual technical system—the teletype network. Likewise, the processing of the data sent from state-owned factories across the country was dependent on the only IBM mainframe computer available to the project in Santiago.

This case may be generalized when it comes to explaining the failures and applications from the *heroic* era of cybernetics: its limited computational capacities were just not yet ready for the implementation of *Big Data* processing in (almost) real-time—e.g., for the simulation of neurological signal processing in the human brain, or what is today called *deep* machine learning, even if artificial intelligence was one of the core concepts developed during the classic cybernetic epoch. What nowadays are celebrated as artificial intelligence, machine learning, process simulations, and neuro-aesthetics, are to a large degree a re-occurrence of cybernetic reasoning, with the only difference being that microprocessors can now achieve the demands of cybernetics.

Heroic Implementing Efforts

As an example, the former Institute for Cybernetics in Paderborn, run by Helmar Frank, coined the notion of "programmed instruction" (*programmierte Instruktion*) for pedagogics in the 1960s to implement not only automated learning in schools, but to replace teachers themselves by an algorithm (Englert et al. 1966). At the very moment when, in the early 1970s, Frank's institute had finally developed a model computer (the MORE) in cooperation with the neighboring computer company Nixdorf—as both learning assistant and didactic object for self-learning (Höltgen 2019; Frank and Meyer 1972)—this TTL-based computer had been surpassed by the first generation of INTEL microchip-based home computers, which were more effective as learning assistants, but conceptually not really conceived as a cybernetic device (Zuther 1996).

Another case is the seminal "tortoise" developed by neurologist William Grey Walter in 1951; an operative demonstration of the core thesis of cybernetics—McCulloch's "experimental epis-temology" (McCulloch 1965)—stating that from a limited number of neurons in the brain, or their equivalent as electro-magnetic relays, complex behavioral patterns emerge. Multiple frictions become evident when trying to re-implement Walter's intent from his archived circuit diagrams. In such a technical demonstration effort, the apparent *collateral* frictions become transparent only by re-enacting Walter's mechanism. When such frictions are read with different, media-archaeological eyes, they rather point to the limits of a brain-computer analogy in a more epistemological sense.[2]

A decisive parameter of these frictions—which occur not simply in the logical, but in the technical implementation of cybernetic diagrams—is their actual temporal behavior. "One important

2   As shown at Humboldt University's Media Theater in 2018 by Juliette Bal's *Tortoise* Juliette, with the local engineering assistance of Ingolf Haedicke.

fact about the computing machine as well as the brain is that
it operates in time" (Wiener 1948, 214)—that is, to be precise,
in *different* times. While the human brain *calculates* in parallel
mode, computing in the Von Neumann architecture operates
strictly sequentially. "As long as we mean by 'parallel' only more
simultaneous discrete operations, I do not think it is the basic
problem" (Pattee 1974, 146). But it is in that "time of non-reality"
(Pias 2003, 158; Pias 2009)[3] that the unconscious flashes up as the
tempoReal.

In 1948, at the outbreak of the Cold War between East and
West, Norbert Wiener defined a transubstantiation in communication engineering: "Information is information, not matter
or energy. No materialism which does not admit this can survive
at the present day" (Wiener [1948] 1961, 132). Socialist countries
collapsed because their economy, for ideological reasons, ana-
chronistically insisted on the priority of matter and energy (Ernst
2013). Still, *applied* cybernetics cannot be reduced to its logical
or mathematical diagram, but it can operatively come into being
only as techno-mathematics, or techno-logics, which makes all
the difference when it comes to frictions. That is why cybernetic
systems cannot be reduced to pure semiotics—that is, symbolical
analysis. The proof of cybernetic reasoning (the pudding) is in
its material implementation (in its eating). The techno-practical
computing being, as an instantiation of orders in the form of
algorithmic programs, is the effective criterion of *computational*
abstraction.

> Many processes in nature must be such that we cannot
> understand them in terms of a computer program and at the
> same time put our understanding to the test by running the
> program on a machine. (Conrad 1995, 279)

3   Wiener revealed his techno-poetic notion of a computational "time of non-
reality" at the 1949 Macy Conference, and this was later problematized by
Pias.

 Against the cybernetic idealism of a seamless modeling of human processes by computing machines, J. C. R. Licklider's seminal text on the human-machine "symbiosis" (Licklider 1960) explicitly points to the differences that arise in the communication between human and non-human agencies. Such frictions do not simply irritate the human-machine *dialogue*, but actually reveal that the dialogic approach is wrong from the beginning. It is from the differences between human reasoning and techno*lógos* that a productive, informative interaction derives.

One of the variables of the frictions which occur when the symbolic order encounters the real is the fully technological machine-machine coupling; a central configuration of cybernetic systems. The media-theoretical techno*lógos* hypothesis states that "the apparently always noisy attempts for bringing such cybernetic systems into full and successful application" (Humboldt-Universität n.d.) is not accidental, but intrinsic to the techno-logical reasoning at work behind its ideal design. This technological reality can be analytically delineated. A central thread of the *Applied Cybernetics* lecture series was "to discuss if, considering the human-machine coupling as the core and hinge of any cybernetic system, the factors that may have truncated the historical deployment of cybernetics remain intrinsic to such core, are external to it, or respond to the articulating quality of such hinge" (Humboldt-Universität n.d.).

In the implementation of cybernetic reasoning, to what extent do the symbolic diagram (or code) and technical matter actually matter? Concerning Chile's Project Cybersyn, in his letter to Stafford Beer from July 13, 1971, Fernando Flores pointed out the *kairotic* (time-critical) moment at which cybernetic thinking may become operative reality, and the opportunity to implement it on a national scale.[4] Beer's first visit to Chile, in November 1971, resulted in flowcharts, notes, and sketches. But against a metaphysical body-mind dichotomy—so familiar to Western

4   See Gómez-Venegas's chapter in this volume.

ontology—radical media archaeology insists that any symbolic operation is already *rooted* in activatable matter—be it the human brain, or electronics. To *en/code* already involves a material medium in the sense of *implementation*—a concept that always includes the options of its realization. It is only by its physical implementation that an abstract algorithm becomes actual software.

Institutionally, cybernetics always oscillated between the rather goal-oriented engineering approach, and a more abstract mathematical system modeling. That is the moment when the specific cultural and social contexts surrounding the application attempt of a particular case must be examined; the moment when either of these approaches were chosen. While the tracing of the discursive, aesthetic, historical and/or political contexts bringing frictions into cybernetic systems is the concern of science and technology studies (Medina 2011), radical media archaeology analyzes the (techno-)epistemological momentum in the actual mate(real)izations, which account for the scope, success, and failures of cybernetics.

One critical aspect in the implementation of the symbolic cybernetic order (feedback-enabled systems) that makes all the difference when transforming the abstract diagram into an operative one (electric circuitry) is the *tempoReal*. This has been expressed in Beer's time-critical approach to economic operations management—in fact inherited from the previous *war theater*. The "vast lag in the receipt of economic data" and the "bureaucratic time it takes to process these data" (Beer [1981] 1994, 248) required, in cybernetic reasoning, to be literally updated in favor of real-time data processing.

Another critical aspect of the encounters of the symbolic order with the *mateReal* is the difference between code (the algorithm) and electronic hardware, which runs parallel to the difference between the Turing Machine's abstract computation, and actual computing. Operational diagrams require a material technological infrastructure, such as a telegraph network, in order to become dynamic cybernetic systems, and acquire negative feedback options in data teleprocessing for the system to control itself—that is, to let its techno*lógos* articulate.

The Cybernetization of Architecture

The architectural design for Ruhr University Bochum in 1960s West Germany was the product of cybernetic systems thinking. The concept failed, to a large degree, precisely due to its material implementation; architecture cannot become cybernetic as long as its building materiality remains unsuitable for recurrent, feedback-based modifications. Only when a symbolic diagram is embedded in concrete matter does it become an actual, operative circuitry. A rejected architectural proposal for Ruhr University by Eckhard Schulze-Fielitz—the Lattice Grid City (*Raumgitterstadt*)—came close to an architectural cybernetics (Bauwelt 1963, 541). "Based on adaptable tubular structures it would form a flexible architecture, that would enable the university to adapt to demand, climate and terrain … a true form of cybernetic architecture as it would have been able to react based on feedback" (van Treeck 2019). This echoes Negroponte's "architecture machine" (1973).

In the planning of Ruhr University's architecture, its underlying diagram aimed "to prioritize informational flows" (van Treeck 2019) by updating the notion of the German university: it sought to open the doors between previously strictly separate academic disciplines, as if they were logical gates in the computer engineering sense. However, frictions between the *lógos* and *techné* of architecture—its actual embodiment—soon took place. Administrative processes may be symbolically expressed in flowcharts, and can thereby be formulated as an algorithm. But actual computing, such as in the *Von Neumann architecture*, differs from macro-spatial building architecture indeed. Concrete architecture cannot itself incorporate the cybernetic techno-logics, since its crucial agency is missing. Feedback is the techno-epistemic core of cybernetic (self)-governance, where output signals regulate the whole process by re-entering the still-running system, either as information in positive (amplifying) or negative (self-regulating) ways. "Maybe architecture when it manifests itself in brick mortar and masses of concrete is not the right medium to incorporate feedback. At best it can facilitate it among the elements that make up the procedural flows it canalizes: people" (van Treeck 2019).

H. T. Odum's Applied Systems Thinking

After World War II—going beyond its military applications such as anti-aircraft prediction—cybernetic systems theory was extended to ecological questions by conceptualizing the feedback loops occurring between the environment and natural resources on the one hand, and in its industrial appropriation on the other (Taylor 1988). The operators of this modeling were theorems, mathematical analysis, and diagrams; its mathematical and material computational episteme was analog computing. Such diagrams became operative technical circuitry in the 1950s and 1960s when H. T. Odum developed "simple electrical networks composed of batteries, wires, resistors and capacitors as models for ecological systems" (Kangas 2004, 101). Circuit diagrams "called passive analogs to differentiate them from operational analog computer circuits, which simulated systems in a different manner" (Kangas 2004, 101). Odum designed a symbolic language to simulate and model ecological and social systems with electronic units such as resistors for delaying, or capacitors for short-term storage. "The language consists of a dozen basic modules, each having a mathematical definition" (Odum 1972, 141). In the sense of operative diagrammatics, "the simulation procedure for the energy circuit follows in simple automatic manner from the energy circuit diagram; the thinking on the behavior and structure of the system is done in the diagramming" (Odum 1972, 210). Odum applied this cybernetic reasoning to a practical teaching program in a signal laboratory: "Students with a yen for the soldering iron can be utilized in combining physical and biological science to make a gadget, which mimics in some ways the flow of materials in the ecosystem" (Odum 1960, 77). But anyone who has ever translated a circuit diagram into real circuitry has experienced the frictions which arise. Actual soldering is, in fact, the most concrete event where the encounter of the symbolic order and *mateReality* take place—a media theory of soldering is still missing (Schulze 2022). What comes close is the symbolic coding of a field-programmable gate array (FPGA) for computer microchips by means of the Very High Speed Integrated Circuit Hardware Description Language (VHDL).

Odum's electrical models became early examples of a technically applied systems ecology, somewhat in parallel to Alban B. Phillips's hydraulic MONIAC (Monetary National Income Analogue Computer) from 1949, preserved in the London Science Museum. The techno*lógos* of such an approach, in the most media-archaeological sense, respects the material embodiment of any kind of symbolic thinking:

> Whereas operational analog methodology involves the writing of differential equations first, passive analog methodology bypasses the equations except to verify the similar behavior of the particular hardware pieces used. The energy network language and the electrical model are forms of mathematics *in themselves*, but forms that naturally resemble the normal ways of thinking in biology, ecology, and the social sciences. (Odum 1971, 261)[5]

To sum up, the question arises: to what extent does a technical realization still relate to its cybernetic conceptualization? The techno-logical frictions that occurred, and still occur, in the efforts of mate(real)izing cybernetic systems, frequently resulting in their failure, are not simply collateral damage, or

5   Emphasis by the author.

noisy disturbances of an otherwise intact reasonable concept. **129**
The material and energetic frictions that take place in *applied*
cybernetics—that is, materially implemented cybernetic system
thinking—have frequently been considered a troublesome
side-effect. Against such an idealistic (techno-)logocentrism, a
different hypothesis has been proposed here: these frictions
are essentially inherent to the techno*lógos* of cybernetics itself.
They deserve to be conceptually included in a techno-materialist
second-order cybernetics. Accordingly, radical media archaeology
pays less attention to the specific cultural and social contexts that
may explain their surrounding conflicts, to focus itself on unrav-
eling their essential role from within technologies themselves.

References

Bauwelt. 1963. "Wettbewerb Universität." *Bauwelt* 19/20: 541.

Beer, Stafford. (1981) 1994. *Brain of the Firm, 2nd Edition*. Chichester: John Wiley &
Sons.

Conrad, Michael. 1995. "The Price of Programmability." In *The Universal Turing
Machine: A Half-Century Survey, Volume 2*, edited by Rolf Herken, 261–81. Vienna/
New York: Springer.

Ernst, Wolfgang. 2013. "Licht im Palast: Eine postmortale Erinnerung an den Code
der DDR." *Tumult* 1: 54–56.

Englert, Ludwig, Helmar Frank, Hans Schiefele, and Herbert Stachowiak, eds. 1966.
Lexikon der kybernetischen Pädagogik und der Programmierten Instruktion. Quick-
born: Schnelle.

Frank, Helmar, and Ingeborg Meyer.1972. *Rechnerkunde: Elemente einer digitalen
Nachrichtenverarbeitung und ihrer Fachdidaktik*. Stuttgart: Kohlhammer.

Höltgen, Stefan. 2019. "Die Aktualisierung kybernetischen Lernens: Der Modell-
rechner des Instituts für Kybernetik im Signallabor der Medienwissenschaft."
Filmed November 2019 in Berlin. YouTube video, 52:16. https://youtu.be/
A9h12vdsaEo.

Humboldt-Universität. n.d. "Applied Cybernetics Lecture Series." Fachgebiet
Medienwissenschaft, Lehrstuhl für Medientheorien. Accessed April 21, 2021.
https://hu.berlin/applied_cybernetics.

Kangas, Patrick. 2004. "The Role of Passive Electrical Analogs in H.T. Odum's
Systems Thinking." *Ecological Modelling* 178 (1-2): 101–06.

Kittler, Friedrich. 1999. *Gramophone, Film, Typewriter*. Stanford: Stanford University
Press.

130 Licklider, Joseph Carl Robnett. 1960. "Man-Computer Symbiosis." *IRE Transactions on Human Factors in Electronics* 1 (1): 4–11. https://doi.org/10.1109/THFE2.1960.4503259.

Medina, Eden. 2011. *Cybernetic Revolutionaries: Technology and Politics in Allende's Chile*. Cambridge: MIT Press.

McCulloch, Warren S. 1965. *Embodiments of Mind*. Cambridge: MIT Press.

Negroponte, Nicholas. 1973. *The Architecture Machine: Toward a More Human Environment*. Cambridge: MIT Press.

Odum, Howard Thomas. 1960. "Ten Classroom Sessions in Ecology." *The American Biology Teacher* 22 (2): 71–78.

———.1971. *Environment, Power, and Society*. New York: Wiley-Interscience.

———. 1972. "An Energy Circuit Language for Ecological and Social Systems: Its Physical Basis." In *Systems Analysis and Simulation in Ecology, Volume 2*, edited by Bernard C. Patten, 139–211. New York: Academic Press.

Pattee, Howard Hunt. 1974. "Discrete and Continuous Processes in Computers and Brains." In *Physics and Mathematics of the Nervous System*, edited by Michael Conrad, Werner Güttinger, and Mario Cin, 128–48. Berlin: Springer.

Pias, Claus. 2009. "Time of Non-Reality: Miszellen zum Thema Zeit und Auflösung." In *Zeitkritische Medien*, edited by Axel Volmar, 267–79. Berlin: Kulturverlag Kadmos.

———, ed. 2003. *Cybernetics: The Macy-Conferences 1946–1953. The Complete Transactions*. Zurich: diaphanes.

Schulze, Malte. 2022. "Löten." In *Medientechnisches Wissen, Band 4: Elektronik, Elektronikpraxis, Computerbau*, edited by Stefan Höltgen, 176–99. Berlin-Boston: De Gruyter.

Tapscott, Don, and Alex Tapscott. 2016. *Blockchain Revolution: How the Technology Behind Bitcoin is Changing Money, Business, and the World*. New York: Penguin Random House.

Taylor, Peter J. 1988. "Technocratic Optimism, H. T. Odum, and the Partial Transformation of Ecological Metaphor after World War II." *Journal of the History of Biology* 21 (2): 213–44.

van Treeck, Jan Claas. 2019. "New Buildings for New Ideas? Ruhr-Universität Bochum and architectural Cybernetics." Paper presented at the workshop Building Communication: Architectural History and Media Archaeology, University of Toronto, McLuhan Centre for Culture and Technology, Toronto, February 8, 2019.

von Clausewitz, Carl. 1832. *Vom Kriege: Hinterlassenes Werk des Generals Carl von Clausewitz*. Berlin: Ferdinand Dümmler.

Wiener, Norbert. 1948. "Time, Communication, and the Nervous System." *Annals of the New York Academy of Sciences* 50 (4): 197–220.

———.(1948) 1961. "Computing Machines and the Nervous System." In *Cybernetics: Or Control and Communication in the Animal and the Machine, 2nd Edition*, 116–32. Cambridge: MIT Press.

Zuther, Friedrich. 1996. *Die Aufhebung der Lehrautomatenentwicklung im Zuge der Entwicklung der Arbeitsplatzrechner*. Aachen: Shaker.

TEACHING MACHINES

MORE

RECHNERKUNDE

HELMAR FRANK

B. F. SKINNER

[6]

Teaching Machines: Learning as Subjective Technique and Feedback Loop

Stefan Höltgen and Rolf F. Nohr

This chapter presents a short media history of teaching machines with a focus on their development at West Germany's Institute for Cybernetics during the 1960s and 1970s. Special media-archaeological attention is paid to the MORE computer and the *Rechnerkunde* approach devised by Helmar Frank and Ingeborg Meyer. Accordingly, this work argues that by tracing the frictions between the USA's perspective on teaching machines—embodied in B. F. Skinner's work—and West Germany's outlook on these systems, contemporary epistemological echoes of teaching machines can be discerned.

We are currently experiencing a boom in the use of digital tools in the educational landscape; not only because of the challenges brought about by the coronavirus pandemic. Apart from their often-improvised use and the recurrent failure of these techno-educational methods—mostly due to the lack of infrastructure and equipment—one notable aspect of this *improvised field test* is the fact that it is not unprecedented. The history of education and media is full of undertakings that sought to produce learning-assistant systems that sometimes aimed to expand and support educational environments. Others, however, simply intended to eliminate the *teaching subject* by automating the production of learning results while making them measurable. In light of the current, technologically-driven teaching scenarios, it seems appropriate to examine the history of automated education, especially considering the mechanisms of self-regulation and automated individual learning that have always been a prom-ising aspect of this history. Therefore, paying attention to the development of teaching machines in the 1950s and 1960s, and to the work of German computer scientist Helmar Frank and his *Institute for Cybernetics* (IfC) in particular, we will argue that the connections between automated learning systems and specific *subject effects* have a deep, *genealogical* dimension. We think that, in order to understand and assess the current debates on educational software, remote teaching, blended learning, and flipped classrooms—especially in relation to results and per-formance—we need to consider the historical constellations that paved the way for the implementation of these techniques.

Teaching Machines

Machine-aided learning systems first emerged in the USA in the mid-1950s, coinciding with the surge of cybernetics, computer-based data processing, mathematics model theory, operations research, and system dynamics. Initially designed as mechanical devices—as opposed to electronic ones—these teaching machines briefly received a lot of attention. They were, at times quite enthusiastically, integrated into schools as well as into the field of science, and were perceived positively by the public. In 1961, *Popular Mechanics* published a report on teaching machines titled *"Will Robots Teach Your Children?"*—a title which could hardly have been further from the truth. The subheading promised "a revolution in mass education": a statement in line with the contemporary discussion on the topic (Bell 1961, 152–57). When they were first used in schools in the USA in the early 1960s, teaching machines were not seen as a means to organize education via an automated third party. Rather, they offered a method to pragmatically help in overcoming the crisis in schools and universities (Foltz 1965, 17)[1] based on autonomous and self-motivated learning approaches. The initial focus was therefore on the course syllabus itself—as opposed to the technology—which was essentially mapped through multiple-choice tests with immediate feedback. Students were seated at a mechanical device (not yet a computer) and tackled the subject matter themselves in an intense question-and-answer process. The devices presented *subject matter segments* followed by a set of questions the student had to answer. If the answers were correct, the device proceeded to the next step; if they were wrong, the subject matter presentation was repeated in iterations of diverse complexity. Students made their way through the syllabus at

---

1   Although a lack of teachers and funding had repeatedly been brought up to justify the necessity of educational reforms, some sources offer a different reason: the West's perception that it lagged behind the achievements of the socialist bloc. In the times of the post-war economy and the looming Cold War, the Western world's need to remain dominant, both in the technological and epistemological spheres, was clear, especially in light of the Sputnik crisis. In Skinner's words: "Our schools, in particular our 'progressive' schools, are often held responsible for many current problems—including juvenile delinquency and the threat of a more powerful foreign technology" (Skinner 1958, 976).

 their own pace, depending on their individual ability to "process knowledge." The iterations—which could potentially be executed endlessly—aimed to ensure the progress of learning. The very fact that teaching machines were both technology- and human-based emphasized the individuality of the learning process, and that the progress of learning could be distinctly measured and processed. However, teaching machines also posit the potential redundancy of a human teaching instance. They embodied the promise of the algorithmization of the learning process, suggesting that traditional teaching formats, subjective teaching styles, as well as collaborative learning could all be suspended. The key notions here—or rather the epistemological discourses supporting the conviction that teaching machines worked—were the ability to condition the learning subject—i.e., behaviorism—and the effectiveness of semi-automated feedback processes and loops during the learning process—i.e., cybernetics. Accordingly, teaching machines were developed for preschoolers and adults, were used in mathematics and language lessons, and were even used to train staff at nuclear missile silos.

Skinner's Machine

The rise of teaching machines coincides with the advancement of modern education and one of its protagonists: Burrhus Frederic Skinner. A representative figure of behaviorism, a discipline to which he contributed substantially, Skinner and this field provided the foundations for programmed learning—which was not merely theoretical. In fact, Skinner worked on developing his own teaching machines. In a seminal essay from 1958, Skinner signals two central developments that, he believed, necessitated the establishment of automated learning: the increasing complexity of tasks in education due to a rising population (Skinner 1958, 969–77) and, on the other hand, the challenge of adapting the educational environment to the technical possibilities of the time—the development of audiovisual media was one of the reasons that made the introduction of teaching machines

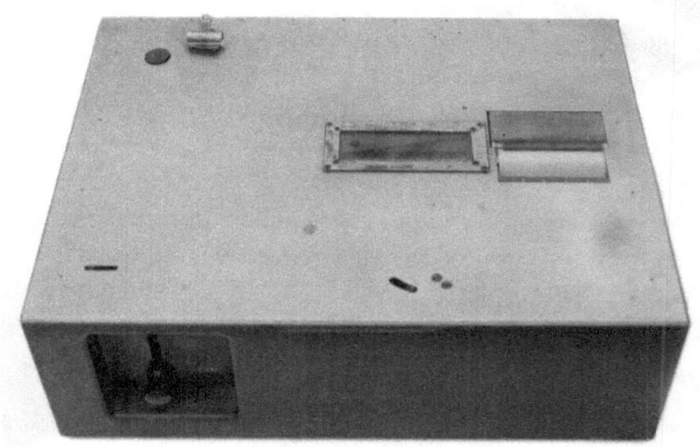

[Fig. 1] B. F. Skinner's early Teaching Machine. Source: image by Silly Rabbit, CC BY 3.0. https://commons.wikimedia.org/w/index.php?curid=3806150.

possible. In his autobiography, Skinner describes the central "enlightening experience" that originally inspired him to take a closer look at teaching machines. He visited his daughter's math class, where he noticed that students did not receive immediate feedback on their performance (Skinner 1983, 64). The class took a test, which the students then handed in, after which it was corrected and given back to them several days later. This, said Skinner, was contrary to the behavioristic theory of learning; the fact that there is no immediate feedback between the test and its correction undermines learning results (Watters 2021, 19). Consequently, Skinner built the prototype of his first machine (fig. 1), which strictly adhered to Pavlov's notions of operant conditioning; when the student provided the correct answer for a question, a bell rang (Watters 2021, 20).

In later developments, Skinner referred to studies that psychologist Sidney L. Pressey had conducted in the late 1920s—Pressey proposed his own programmed learning system, but initially had no public success (Skinner 1958, 969; Benjamin 1988, 703). Starting from his theory of learning, and closely following

 Edward L. Thorndike's approaches on "instrumental conditioning" (Niemiec and Walberg 1989, 265), Pressey developed a simple test device that required students to answer questions by pressing buttons, providing immediate feedback on their inputs. In 1926, Pressey himself summarized the results of his work at Ohio State University: the immediacy of the feedback would fix the correct answer to the subject's memory, and the device could be adapted to give out candy or other forms of reward when the student reached a specific level. This confirmation of achievement would have "cemented the learning results" (Pressey 1960, 37; Watters 2021, 61–80).

In his interpretation of Pressey's work, Skinner understood that machines for programmed learning would both *test* and *evaluate*, and at the same time, they would trigger actual learning processes. These processes would also be characterized, to a considerable extent, by the individualization of the learning process,[2] resulting in an "industrial revolution in education" (Skinner 1958, 969).[3] However, Skinner goes beyond Pressey's work by redefining the learning process itself; that is, a modification of emitted changes in behavior, rather than a mere conveyance of knowledge. For Skinner, this made the machine a secondary actor compared to the actual "knowledge-changing program" (Niemiec and Walberg 1989, 266).

Beyond the apparent similarity with the Taylorian principle of increasing effectiveness, which was popular at the time (Niemiec and Walberg 1989, 264), the underlying notion of behavioristic

2   Whereas individualization is initially seen as a learning process and not as a self-technique: "The kind of individual difference which arises simply because a student has missed part of an essential sequence (compare the child who has no 'mathematical ability' because he was out with the measles when fractions were first taken up) will simply be eliminated" (Skinner 1958, 976).

3   Other sources point to the emergence of computers and computing culture, as well as to the general scientifization of learning and decision-making processes, as the origin of this revolution (Czemper and Boswau 1965, 37).

learning (Lumsdaine 1959, 164) is key to understanding the
teaching machines movement. In the discussion on teaching
machines, the learning effect is usually understood as part of
operant conditioning, characterized by an almost immediate,
individualized feedback on learning results, or to be more precise, on the correctness of the answers (Foltz 1965, 41). This is the
predominant way of thinking of behaviorism, where observable,
empiric, and unambiguous human (and animal) reactions are
traced back to environmental stimuli. The black box metaphor
is a typical example of this: the interior structure of the studied
object is initially of no interest; a demonstrable connection
between input and output is key. In the concrete case of teaching
machines, this input is specific teaching content combined with
the size of the class, the age of the students, and the duration of
the teaching session; the output is the measured success of the
learning process (Zöller 1975, 99).

In the 1960s, this *operant* conceptualization of the learning
process brought about two schools of thought on programmed
learning processes based on instructional devices: the Skinner
school and the Crowder school (Fry 1963, 17-34)—Norman A.
Crowder was the vice president and technical director of the
Educational Science Division of the US Industries. These two
types of learning programming differed in how they conceived
the role of repetition. Both emphasized the effectiveness of
repeated messages and questions for the lessons to be learned.
Skinner's *linear program*, however, focused itself on small details
of the questions, on the answers phrased by the students,
and on the progress of learning, advancing in tiny steps—all in
the spirit of the operant conditioning approach to learning. In
contrast, Crowder's *branching programming* emphasized the
explicit effect of mistakes. They would lead the student into
enhanced repetitive routines and would simultaneously—by
a more strongly branching algorithm architecture—guarantee
an "intrinsic" (Fry 1963, 5) adaptation of the student's individual
level of knowledge (Vogt 1966, 40-43). Based more strongly

 on Pressey's work, Crowder favored multiple-choice tests with immediate feedback. This made him the target of criticism stating that, ultimately, his method came close to mere "test and quiz questions" (Deutsch 1964, 44). Eventually, the Skinner school of thought prevailed:

> [Skinner] had produced more than a machine; he had developed an educational technology that promoted a new approach to teaching … The boom in teaching machines was underway in the early 1960s, and most of the devices were based on Skinner's theory of learning. (Benjamin 1988, 709)

Booms

Skinner's bell-ringing teaching machine, and the *rediscovery* of Pressey's work thus marked the beginning of the boom in teaching machines (Niemiec and Walberg 1989, 264). In 1962, US educational psychologist Robert Glaser introduced the term "instructional system," (Glaser 1962, 1–30) focusing on teaching machines and programmed learning. In 1965, psychologist and educator Robert Gagné published his book *The Conditions of Learning* ([1965] 1970), which quickly became a great success, constituting a paradigmatic work on teaching theory, and sparking broad attention to instructional design. In 1962, Charles I. Foltz published *The World of Teaching Machines: Programmed Learning and Self-Instructional Devices*. The book is a fundamental work within the teaching machines movement; however, according to the introduction, Foltz opted for a wait-and-see attitude and tried not to be too enthusiastic when talking about the matter. All the same, by the mid-1960s a proper market had developed: Foltz estimated that by around 1965 there were approximately 40 to 50 manufacturers of learning devices, plus another 20 companies publishing textbooks and syllabi for them. Accordingly, he calculated that the expected turnover for the following 10 years in this sector would amount to US$100 million (Foltz 1965, 47). In parallel, a research funding program sponsored by both state-run and private institutions—e.g., the Carnegie Corporation, Ford Foundation—was launched, aiming to support fundamental research at universities on this matter (Czemper and Boswau 1965, 88).

As the ambitions of the parties involved increasingly moved towards slide projection, film-supported (Lumsdaine and May 1958), and computer-based interpretation of the teaching methodology, during the second phase of the short teaching machine boom, there was a rise in the cooperation between universities and hardware manufacturers within the computer industry. These cooperative programs were usually grouped under the term of "computer-assisted instruction," or other programs promoted by the US government, such as the Center for Programmed Instruction run by the US Department of Education (Molnar 1990, 80–83; Niemiec and Walberg 1989). In this context, the Minnesota Educational Computing Consortium (MECC) is worth mentioning. Along with Total Information for Education Systems, founded by Dale LaFrenz and others in 1968, the MECC established a computer network that used modems to connect suburban schools in the greater Minneapolis area to mainframe computers. The network was used to provide learning software and automated learning assistant systems to schoolchildren for decades. One of the most successful and renowned MECC learning programs was *The Oregon Trail* from 1972. A simulation of the Western US during the 1840s, it was for many US citizens one of their first contacts with computer games, and it is considered a *classic* video game to this day (Google, n.d.).

However, we do not want to focus the discussion here on the expansion of teaching machines to think tanks, the emerging computer industry, or the general debate on automation and control. Rather, we are interested in the debate teaching machines triggered in Germany, and the specific scenario this produced.

One of the key institutions in the development of teaching machines and information psychology in West Germany was the Institute for Cybernetics (IfC). Established at the University of Pedagogics in Berlin (*Pädagogische Hochschule zu Berlin*) on August 28, 1964 and headed by Helmar Frank, this was the first institute at a German university to deal with cybernetic pedagogy (Lehnert 1969, 3). "Accordingly, one of the primary goals of cybernetic pedagogy is to objectify certain intellectual achievements performed by educators, i.e., to delegate them to cybernetic machines developed for this specific purpose" (Lehnert 1969, 3).[4] Although the institute was linked to the Association for Programmed Instruction (*Gesellschaft für Programmierte Instruktion*, GPI), it insisted on developing, at least to a certain extent, its own approach to cybernetics. The GPI, on the other hand, was a scientific umbrella association that

> brought together researchers and practitioners from the fields of programmed instruction, language laboratories, and remote transmission didactics (e.g., educational TV). The association deserves particular credit for succeeding in attracting scientists from all four possible fields of programmed instruction. Whether they represent[ed] the liberal arts (Prof. Zielinski), cybernetics (Prof. H. Frank; Prof. K. Weltner), empirical pragmatism or behaviorism (Prof. W. Correll) the GPI not only respect[ed] but welcome[d] their views. (Heyder 1965)

The differences between the Berlin Institute for Cybernetics and the GPI may illustrate how cybernetic pedagogy differentiated itself from the range of operational approaches to programmed instruction and the discourse on teaching machines. Nonetheless, both institutions—along with the Center for Educational Technology (*Bildungstechnologisches Zentrum*) in Wiesbaden— broke ground in the development of teaching machines and programmed instruction in Germany. The fact that the IfC had cooperated with local computer companies and was equipped with its own computer center—initially sponsored by Siemens

4   All translations by the authors.

through an S-303-P system, and later by Nixdorf with four N-820
computers (Lehnert 1969, 4)—offers a particularly relevant
thread.

Helmar Frank and the Institute for Cybernetics

Cybernetician Helmar Frank turned to information aesthetics
early on, which later became the theoretical foundation of his
cybernetic pedagogy. Writing his doctoral thesis on this subject in
Stuttgart in the late 1950s (Frank 1959), he was part of the scene
where Max Bense transferred information aesthetics to practical
and theoretical computer art projects. After completing his
doctorate, Frank initially investigated teaching machines in Karlsruhe as part of Karl Steinbuch's group, before being appointed
professor for information science at the University of Pedagogics
in Berlin in 1963. There, he transferred his theoretical preliminary
considerations on information aesthetics to pedagogy, defining
his future field of work in the book *Cybernetic Foundations of Pedagogics* (*Kybernetische Grundlagen der Pädagogik*) from 1962. In
the late 1960s, Frank moved from Berlin to Paderborn, where he
led the recently-established Research and Development Center
for Objectified Educational Methods (*Forschungs- und Entwick-
lungszentrum für objektivierte Lehr- und Lernverfahren*, FEoLL),
and founded the Institute for Cybernetics. In Paderborn, Frank
also pursued a political strategy, as West Germany planned to
establish an IT center there in cooperation with the computer
manufacturer Nixdorf and the new local university.

Accordingly, Frank and his colleagues focused their work on
materializing his initial theoretical considerations, which was
done with a double emphasis: "*constructive* and *empirical* work to
produce computer-related material as a school subject" (Frank
and Meyer 1972, 23).[5] For this, Frank decided to describe all

5   Emphasis by the authors.

144 processes as cybernetic feedback operations, thus setting the basis both for didactics in general, as well as for his *Rechnerkunde* (Computer Science)—the very first example of computer science teaching in Germany: "the computer is introduced on two levels of observation: first as an educational object that the reader will *become familiar* with, and secondly as an educational object that he will learn to *teach to*" (Frank and Meyer 1972, 23). This learning process takes place as a dialog between humans and machines, during which each learns from the other. This, however, meant that one must have a precise understanding of the machine in order to be taught by it. That is why Frank begins his *Rechnerkunde* with a section on what is today known as computer engineering, before moving onto practical computer science. This resulted in an inductive learning process:

> From a didactic point of view, using problem-oriented pro-gramming languages (Algol, Fortran, Cobol, etc.) to intro-duce students to data processing is the incorrect approach, as they cloud, if not completely obstruct, our view of the objectification conducted by the computer. When learners have attempted to program a computer using machine code or machine-oriented code, and have thus familiarized themselves with the computer's functionality, they do not need (and at the same time will not have the necessary knowledge) to learn higher programming languages. (Frank and Meyer 1972, 21)

Nevertheless, a central aspect of Frank's cybernetic pedagogy is that his *Rechnerkunde* does not constitute an end by itself. Rather, it gives learners an entry point to the study of cybernetics. Frank understood computers as models that could help in exemplifying cybernetic principles, calling them, accordingly, MORE; a German abbreviation for model computer (*Modell-Rechner*). Before out-lining these model machines, a brief overview of the MORE pro-gram and its predecessors is required.

BAKKALAUREUS is the acronym for "Modular System of Combinable Cybernetic Machines which Performs Autonomous and Computer-Supported Examination and Educational Work" (*Baukastensystem aus kombinierbaren kybernetischen Automaten leistet autonom und rechnerunterstützt Examinier- und Schulungsarbeit*) (Frank 1969, 45). The devices using this modular system were developed in Berlin and Paderborn between 1964 and 1973. We argue that their rising complexity simultaneously offers insights into the development of German teaching machines, and shows the successive and increasing influence that digital and computer technology had in this field in Germany.

[Fig. 2] BAKKALAUREUS program at the 1973 Didacta trade fair for the education sector. Source: authors' personal archive.

Introduced in 1970, the ETS/e system was a typewriter with a modified keyboard. A Nixdorf N-820 computer could lock or release the keys via remote control, meaning that the ETS/e could be used for multiple-choice questions. Most early teaching-learning devices within the BAKKALAUREUS program sought to technically support multiple-choice questions (Frank 1975, 89). Although true interactivity between these devices and users had been the main goal of cybernetic didactics since the outset, it was not realized until digital computers were integrated.

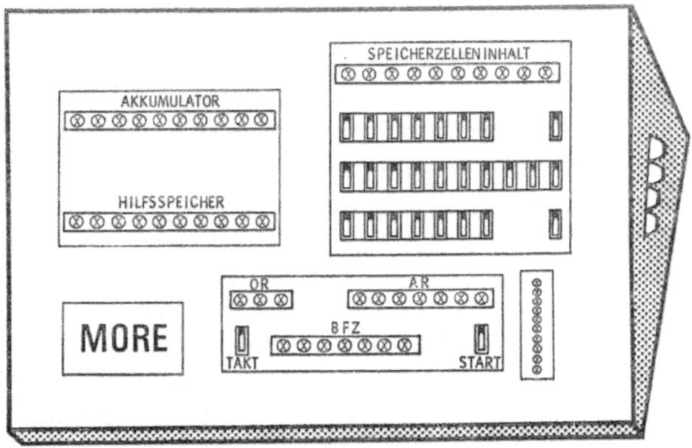

[Fig. 3] Schematic illustration of the model computer (MORE). Source: authors' personal archive.

The GEROMAT system, funded by the Volkswagen Foundation and developed in Berlin, was realized in four iterations between 1964 and 1970, and was also part of the BAKKALAUREUS program (Thomas 2006, 42–44). The system had a multimedia supplement for language laboratories with the following components:

- ROBBIMAT: a multi-station testing system controlled by a central teaching unit.
- DIDACT: an individual training device with a display unit. Films, slides, and photographs had to be inserted into the device by hand.
- MITSI: an add-on unit which made audio information available.
- ROBBIMAT III: the highest expansion level of the system. A Nixdorf N-820 computer that controlled all the training devices as a "master computer" (Frank 1975, 57), but which was rarely used due to its high price.

The Nixdorf N-820 computer was, however, used again for the ITERATOR system; an emulator of a model computer for 30 learners. Similarly, the MORE (fig. 3) was initially only a *concept* computer—a model computer in both senses of the word. The archive of the Institute for Cybernetics contains comprehensive

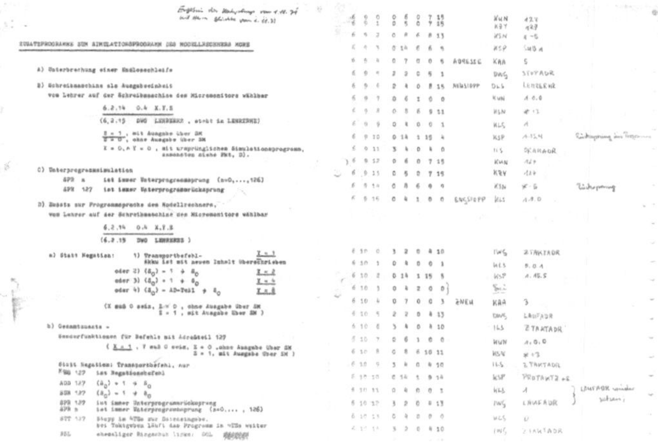
ZUSATZPROGRAMME ZUM SIMULATIONSPROGRAMM DES MODELLRECHNERS MORE

A) Unterbrechung einer Endlosschleife

B) Schreibmaschine als Ausgabeeinheit
vom Lehrer auf der Schreibmaschine des Micromonitors wählbar

6.2.14 0.4 X.Y.Z

(6.2.15 DWO LEHRERKZ , steht in LEHRERKZ)

Z = 1 , mit Ausgabe über SM
Z = 0 , ohne Ausgabe über SM
X = 0 ∧ Y = 0 , mit ursprünglichem Simulationsprogramm, ansonsten siehe Pkt. D).

C) Unterprogrammsimulation
SPR n ist immer Unterprogrammsprung (n=0,...,126)
SPR 127 ist immer Unterprogrammrücksprung

D) Zusatz zur Programmsprache des Modellrechners,
vom Lehrer auf der Schreibmaschine des Micromonitors wählbar

6.2.14 0.4 X.Y.Z

(6.2.15 DWO LEHRERKZ)

a) Statt Negation: 1) Transportbefehl- Akku ist mit neuem Inhalt überschrieben X = 1
oder 2) $(a_0) - 1 \rightarrow a_0$ X = 2
oder 3) $(a_0) + 1 \rightarrow a_0$ X = 4
oder 4) (a_0) - AD-Teil $\rightarrow a_0$ X = 8

[Fig. 4] Excerpt from the MORE emulator program in the N-820 assembler. Source: Archive of the Institute for Cybernetics. Courtesy of the Deutsches Technikmuseum Berlin.

materials on the MORE simulation; among them, a 100-page printout of the N-820's assembler listings (fig. 4) which provides information on the computer's working principles. However, a mere emulation of the MORE would have contradicted Frank's own demands; namely, that discovering a "computer's functionality" via programming entailed that it would not be the computer which would be programmed. Consequently, two of Frank's collaborators, Dr. Sommer and Dr. Closhen, built an actual MORE computer, which they finished in the spring of 1970 (Frank and Lehnert 1973, 25). Ingeborg Meyer, a female student of pedagogics who worked at the IfC, used that computer as the basis to design a practical computer science course. Reports on *Rechnerkunde* courses using the MORE can be found until the mid-1970s. They include field reports written by Dr. Simons (1973 and 1975); a syllabus titled *Rechnerkunde Course A/B Using the MORE,* developed by G. Lobin (1973); worksheets for students and evaluation forms of Meyer's *Rechnerkunde Course C* (n.d.); and the book *Rechnerkunde* itself, written by Meyer and Frank.

Technical-Didactic Reductions with the MORE

The prototype of a MORE computer used for this chapter[6]—part of the IfC archive—is a type of machine known as a TTL computer. There, the system's CPU is not a single component, but a "dissolved" set of individual logic modules (TTL) of the 74 series. These are integrated circuits containing several digital logic gates, which have been repeatedly used in circuit implementations since the 1960s (Texas Instruments 1972). Given that the types of integrated circuits are easily identifiable—the date of manufacture was printed on them—it is possible to narrow down the date on which this MORE prototype was created: the oldest component is from 1973, meaning the prototype could not have been built before this date.

The MORE was designed as a binary 10-bit computer in accordance with the Von Neumann architecture: 7 bits were used for addressing—resulting in a maximum addressable storage of 128 bytes—and 3 bits for instructions—which allowed up to eight instructions. The computer offered two clock speeds: 2 and 4 hertz. It was programmed using switches and binary machine code, and the data output was represented, as binary values, with LED lights. The MORE was initially programmed on paper. Programs were written as mnemonic code, which were then manually translated into machine code—chains of zeros and ones. Thus, programmers obtained detailed knowledge on the construction of machine instructions.

6   The MORE was studied through a series of workshops and research projects led by Stefan Höltgen and Marius Groth at the Signal Lab of the Institute of Media Science of Humboldt-Universität zu Berlin between 2017 and 2019.

[Fig. 5] MORE punch-card reader. Source: authors' personal archive.

As its main memory, the MORE has a punch card reader through which programs and data could be loaded but not stored (fig. 5). Despite having only eight *opcodes*—instruction machine codes— the MORE has every function of a Turing-complete code; that is, the computer could be programmed for any task, and could thus be used to this day as a *didactically-reduced* model computer equivalent to any kind of Turing-complete digital computer according to the Von Neumann architecture.

Rechnerkunde

The MORE's role is expanded in the *Rechnerkunde* pedagogics. In their book, Frank and Meyer present five steps, all using the MORE, to "scientifically examine the phenomenon of computers" (Texas Instruments 1972, 13):

1. The philosophical step: logic; particles of thought; implementation.
2. The algorithmic step: human thought as an algorithm; objectification processes.

Type EMF 2000

Type EMT 2000

[Fig. 6] MORE brochure published by ELFE (front). Source: authors' personal archive.

3. The engineering and cybernetics step: physical-chemical realization; computer technology.
4. The research-organizational scientific step: computers as tools in research, society, and media technology.
5. The business and social science step: changing production conditions through computers.

University-level computer science courses usually cover steps two and three, but according to Frank and Meyer, their *Rechnerkunde* already dealt with all five steps at a high-school level. This was possible thanks to the didactic-technical reduction implemented in their computer and its simple design, which was intended to be mass produced after a trial period. The MORE would be built by the Berlin-based teaching machines company ELFE (fig. 6). However, beyond brochures, we have been unable to find substantial information about this company—except for the advertisement of the EMF 2000 model computer (a wall-installed demonstration machine), and the EMT 2000 (a small device for students), as well as templates of the latter machine, which could actually be used for programming exercises.

Rechnerkunde also describes the MORE's construction, its functionality, and programming, and elaborates on the computer's educational scope. According to Frank and Meyer, *Rechnerkunde* classes should use six main questions as guidelines:

6. What is being taught: the scope and structure of the subject matter (S).
7. Who is being taught: the learners' psychological structure (P).
8. Why is the subject matter being taught: the educational objective (O) the teaching machine is aimed at.
9. Additional, foreseeable, stimulating, or disrupting socio-cultural influences (I) that will probably emerge.[7]
10. What objects are used to teach the subject matter: the media configuration (M) being used. In particular, the MORE and its add-ons (protective covers, readers, etc.).
11. The educational strategy (E) according to which the subject matter is being taught. (Frank and Lehnert 1972, 28–30).

These six questions structured the *Rechnerkunde* didactics, which Frank formally explained thus: I, M, P, O, and S are condition fields, and E is the decision field in which didactic decisions can be made. Hence, for a given teaching method, the combination of these variables formed the D function, being expressed by Frank, for example, as DIMPOSMORE or D32MORE—where 32 des-ignates didactic function number 32 in a set of 63 possible ways to distribute the six educational variables across the two subsets of condition and decision fields. This formal description is also at the basis of the *Rechnerkunde* teaching program (Frank and Lehnert

---

7   This question is not just interesting because it hints at the Shannon-Weaver model of communication, but also because the IfC used it to justify the use of Esperanto in its teaching, arguing that by employing a new language to learn about other subject matters, students would be free from the inter-ference of their mother tongues (metaphors, double meanings, etc.) during the learning process.

 1972, 32) where Frank introduces the MORE in accordance with the following principles:

- Elementary introduction to digital message processing (Frank)
- Binary code
- Dual arithmetic
- Logical functions and Boolean algebra
- Adders
- Computer architecture
- External program control (state machine)
- Internal program control (Turing machine)
- Transfer to current commercial computers
- Teaching methodology approach to Rechnerkunde (Meyer)

Lessons should include the MORE as quickly as possible to help exemplify theoretical teaching in practice. Furthermore, students should incorporate the lessons learned into possible applications with the MORE, through which they would learn how to code by trial and error.

Single-Board Teaching Computers

In the late 1960s and early 1970s, the teaching machines of the Institute for Cybernetics represented promising technologies. At the 1973 Didacta trade fair (fig. 2), the MORE and the BAKKALAUREUS program were in effect presented as the teaching technologies of the future—not just for the field of computer science. Moreover, according to our findings both projects were implemented at vocational schools and high schools in and around Paderborn and Berlin. When microprocessor technology began to dominate the market from the mid-1970s on, computers became so affordable that schools were able to purchase them in large quantities, and technological progress itself "canceled" the Institute for Cybernetics' systems:

> The workstation computer with the appropriate equipment actually appears to be a universal teaching machine. Its current possibilities exceed those of the former teaching

[Fig. 7] Signetics Instructor 50. Source: authors' personal archive.

automats by far. Teaching machines benefit from all the ergonomic features of the workstation computers (graphic user interfaces, voice input and output, high-resolution graphic screens, etc.). (Zuther 1996, 101)

The MORE system, *which* from a didactic perspective was open, was then gradually replaced by *closed* microcomputers which brought about an important shift in *Rechnerkunde*. Basically, it was turned inside-out: computer science didactics has since then departed from machine-centric and bottom-up approaches, favoring problem-oriented teaching, which take the user interface as their starting point (Höltgen 2016, 141–51). However, both the MORE's architecture and textbooks on single-board computers—e.g., SEL-Z80 Trainer—show that the didactic and technical principles of cybernetic pedagogy and the MORE are by no means outdated. Today, the technical principles of that small teaching computer can still be found in the form of afford-able systems, such as Arduino, Calliope, and the Raspberry Pi, and small build-it-yourself TTL computers such as the Gigatron or the Instructor 50 (fig. 7). The fact that the incremental black-boxing of computers—through miniaturization, networking, and virtualization on the user's side, and vertical technological dif-ferentiation on the manufacturer's side—had revived old forms of curiosity (Höltgen 2022, 204), can be considered, we contend, a comeback of cybernetic pedagogy. It is a curiosity that reviving *Rechnerkunde* and its epistemological approach is nowadays expressed in the hacking, making, and repairing of computers.

Conclusion

This short history of teaching machines and their shift from the USA to West Germany shows how distinct their underlying discourse became. Starting with a simple conceptualization of teaching mechanisms as a form of operant conditioning, an understanding of the learning process as a type of self-mon-itoring feedback loop quickly developed. This in turn led to an increasing reassessment of *performance* as the goal of teaching machines. In Germany, the latent *cybernetization* of these systems yielded a coupling between specialized educational content and teaching machines, giving birth to a sort of meta-system where both form and content became congruent. So, what caused the failure of this brief boom in teaching machines? Pointing to the fact that the brilliant and successful educational projects their creators anticipated had failed to materialize seems to us to be too narrow a viewpoint. We think that addressing the slightly more abstract issues teaching machines produced—e.g., their "control-political" effects—is a more productive strategy.

Even during the early phase of teaching machines in the US, it became clear that there were *frictions* between reality and the extreme functionality of the methods employed. One major point of criticism addressed behaviorism's understanding of learning, and thus its associated conceptualization of humanity—which did not view learning as a subjective process. Instead, behaviorism viewed the subjects being taught—in the context of a stimulus-response *external governing*—as an overly-individual, manageable component of the process. This reduced subjects to *learning objects* that were no longer subject to their own will. Moreover, a debate emerged around the frictions between teaching programs and machines: the oft-cited phrase "the program is everything, the learning machine nothing," summarizes the criticism of so-called "page-turning machines" (Deutsch 1964, 39). This appraisal considered that using teaching machines in complex learning situations—e.g., industrial vocational training—would make students feel *patronized* by machines, resulting in a tendency to disobey them (Schirm 1964, 132). In this respect, teaching machines may be seen as the systemic reaction to a stage of crisis—i.e., lack of teachers, new challenges in education, the Sputnik crisis—at the core of which lie the consequences of a politics of control (Scheskakow 1965; Vogt 1966).[8]

In Germany, the development of teaching machines proved less crisis-driven and more a consequence of the increasing role of science in governance from the 1940s on. "Regulate what can be regulated; ensure anything that cannot be regulated becomes regulable" (Schmidt 1941, 81). In line with the notion of predictability, which was a topic of discussion in the UK at around the same time, teaching machines seemed to be a sort of utopian answer to the question of whether teaching processes could be fully automated. This utopian promise was finally fulfilled when teaching machines were replaced by *other* machines—Turing machines. Microcomputers entered schools in the second half of the 1970s, replacing the BAKKALAUREUS machines and continuing the MORE's legacy. The fact that this had introduced new technological obstacles that in turn swung the pendulum

8   The fact that learning machines were developed and used in socialist countries is proof that this crisis of control was not just a Western problem (Schestakow 1965).

 from *the real* to *the symbolic*—from hardware to programming languages—moved the discourse of computer science to other teaching methods.

To some, teaching machines may seem antiquated, not sufficiently complex or effective, and even almost naive. But what distinguishes teaching machines from today's software-based learning projects? Language learning tools such as Duolingo, the brief boom in open content for university lectures, and classroom tools, all essentially use the same mechanisms as those present in the realm of teaching machines. Drawing a line that goes from the *teaching machines* of the 1950s, passes through the self-instructional learning model of the 1960s, and arrives at today's debates on gamification seems to be the logical description of the evolution of the field. Nonetheless, the different apparatus and architecture of semi-automated learning systems appear to have developed a life of their own, beyond their intended action-rational functionality. The learning process that uses *ludic methods* and self-regulating features becomes a process that seems constantly threatened by "*the game.*" Skinner had already talked about a *pinball-machine effect*, observing that, beyond the programmed educational content, the learning machine itself interrupts the student's gaming operation. Similar to pinball machines, there is a risk, Skinner argued, of interactions with the learning machine that challenge the gaming operation to such an extent that the student's will to beat the machine—i.e., winning the game—could become more dominant than the learning process itself. "The negative aspect of the innovative effect … is that most children are so highly motivated that they would rather conquer or cheat the machine in play than learn from it" (Foltz 1965, 47).

In a word, insights on the connection between learning subjects and teaching machines, on the technology used for this purpose, and on the epistemology of cybernetics can be derived from these pages. In this sense, the reward which learning subjects receive from teaching machines would not merely be the

acquisition of knowledge, but also an ostensible experience of
self-empowerment and self-efficacy. At the core of the project
on teaching machines there is a (rather naive) image of learning
subjects as individuals who are not controlled by superordinate,
teleological logic—or processed by a learning algorithm. Instead,
they would use their own intuitive capacity to act, thus developing learning results intuitively based on pre-structured
processes. Regarding the discourse on teaching machines,
however, it would make more sense to understand acting subjects as connected subjects; as entities that can be addressed
through the educational tool of the game. This self-determined
learning is twice as effective because these game-like processes
create an experience within which training and development
reach a high level of effectiveness, given that the subjects in this
context are self-motivated, adapting themself voluntarily—and
because their performance becomes measurable.

Nonetheless, the gamification of learning has been fruitful,
although outside the regulations of syllabi. In hacker spaces,
coding dojos, and repair cafés, the old black boxes called
computers are repeatedly transformed into a new subject matter,
and are learned through the cybernetic-autodidactic methods
of trial and error, and learning by doing. In an effort to acquire
the knowledge hidden within the technology, a subversive epistemology started spreading in the late 1950s, leading to some
of the findings discussed in this chapter. In that vein, before the
MORE documentation was found in the uncatalogued estate of
the IfC, the device itself was scrutinized (see footnote 6). Consequently, by teaching about and through the device, fully in the
spirit of Frank's *Rechnerkunde*, the experimenters learned from
the device, deriving the didactics behind it.

In the context of this book, therefore, teaching machines provide
a self-evident insight into the question of *frictions*. On the one
hand, they provided an approach which understood that these
systems would amount to the pure implementation of previously
devised theories and models—the one embodied in Skinner's

 work. On the other, they provided a perspective that found, at the very technological depths of these machines, lessons that would *inform* the teaching-learning process. In brief, these views allow one to trace two essentially frictional agencies: one aiming at using teaching machines as the instruments for the deployment of a program; the other letting the program be the product of technological processes itself. It may thus be argued that the first approach, always at odds with the episteme machines produced, played a relevant role in the decline of teaching machines. However, such an argument does not acknowledge, for example, that Frank's undertaking—representative of the second per-spective—was also affected by not understanding the modes and rhythms by which the episteme of machines unfolds. Does the battle between TTL computers and microprocessors mentioned above not speak to this? Perhaps the *frictions*-motivated method of analysis allows us to verify that one of the main insights we can get from the age of cybernetics is that, at the bottom of complex technological systems, a new sort of knowledge is being devel-oped: one that tends to escape the control of humans, giving way, for example, to the *everlasting life* of teaching machines, now con-cretized in gamification systems or open microcomputer sets that continue to inform our modes of learning and knowledge.

References

Bell, Joseph N. 1961. "Will Robots Teach Your Children?" *Popular Mechanics* (October): 152–57.

Benjamin, Ludy T. 1988. "A History of Teaching Machines." *American Psychologist* 43 (9): 703–12.

Czemper, Karl-Achim, and Herbert Boswau. 1965. *Unterricht und Computer: Die Anwendung elektronischer Rechenanlagen in der amerikanischen Pädagogik*. Munich: Oldenbourg.

Deutsch, Jürgen R.H. 1964. "Stand der technischen Entwicklung von Lehrmaschinen in der deutschen Industrie." In *Programmierter Unterricht und Lehrmaschinen: Bericht Internationale Konferenz*, edited by Armand Bianchérie, Ernst R. Hilgard, Harry M. B. Hurwitz, P. Kenneth Komoski, Gerald A. Randell, Halmuth Schaefer, and Walter Schultze, 37–50. Berlin: Pädagogische Arbeitsstelle.

Foltz, Charles I. 1965. *Lehrmaschinen. Geräte, Programme, Anwendungsbereiche.* Weinheim: Beltz.

Frank, Helmar, and Ingeborg Meyer. 1972. *Rechnerkunde. Elemente der digitalen Nachrichtenverarbeitung und ihrer Fachdidaktik.* Stuttgart: Kohlhammer.

Frank, Helmar, and Uwe Lehnert. 1973. *Institut für Kybernetik, Berlin—Paderborn: Ein Rückblick auf ein Jahrzehnt kybernetisch-pädagogischer Forschungs-, Entwicklungs- und Aufklärungsarbeit.* Paderborn: Institut für Kybernetik.

Frank, Helmar. 1959. "Grundlagenprobleme der Informationsästhetik und erste Anwendung auf die mime pure." PhD diss., Technische Hochschule Stuttgart.

———.1962. *Kybernetische Grundlagen der Pädagogik: Kybernetik und Information Series, Volume 2.* Baden-Baden and Paris: Agis/Gauthier-Villars.

———.1969. *Kybernetische Grundlagen der Pädagogik, Volume 2.* Baden-Baden: Agis.

———.1975. *Neue Bildungsmedien und -technologien in der Schul- und Berufsaus- bildung. Mit einer kritischen Stellungnahme von Felix von Cube (Schriften der Kom- mission für wirtschaftlichen und sozialen Wandel Nr. 58).* Göttingen: Schwartz & Co.

Fry, Edward B. 1963. *Teaching Machines and Programed Instruction: An Introduction.* New York: McGraw-Hill.

Gagné, Robert Mills. (1965) 1970. *Die Bedingungen des menschlichen Lernens.* Han- over: Schroedel.

Glaser, Robert, ed. 1962. *Training Research and Education.* New York: Columbia Uni- versity Press.

Google. n.d. "The Oregon Trail, MECC, and the Rise of Computer Learning." Accessed September 11, 2021. https://artsandculture.google.com/exhibit/ TAICA30JZQm2Kw.

Heyder, Gunther. 1965. "Kellerkind Kybernetik: Professor Franks neues Institut ist in arger Geldnot." *Die Zeit*, December 3, 1965.

Höltgen, Stefan. 2016. "GO BACK GOTO: Ein kurzer Rückblick auf die Entfernung der Schulinformatik von den Computern." *GRGK* 57 (3): 141–51.

———.2022. *OPEN HISTORY: Archäologie des Retrocomputings.* Berlin: Kulturverlag Kadmos.

Lehnert, Uwe. 1969. "Portrait: Institut für Kybernetik, PH Berlin." *ARCH+* 2 (6): 3–6.

Lumsdaine, Arthur A. 1959. "Teaching machines and self-instructional materials." *Audio-Visual Communication Review* 7 (1): 163–81.

Lumsdaine, Arthur A., and Robert Glaser, eds. 1960. *Teaching Machines and Programmed Learning I: A Source Book.* Washington D.C.: National Education Association.

Lumsdaine, Arthur A., and Mark A. May. 1958. *Learning from Films.* New Haven: Yale University Press.

Molnar, Andrew. 1990. "Computers in Education: A Historical Perspective of the Unfinished Task." *T|H|E Journal* 18 (4): 80–83.

Niemiec, Richard P., and Herbert J. Walberg. 1989. "From Teaching Machines to Microcomputers: Some Milestones in the History of Computer-Based Instruction." *Journal of Research on Computing in Education* 21 (3): 263–76.

160 Nohr, Rolf F. 2019. *Unternehmensplanspiele 1955–1975: Die Herstellung unternehmerischer Rationalität im Spiel. Unter Mitarbeit von Tobias Conradi, Tim Glaser, Kerstin Hoffmann und Theo Röhle*. Münster: Lit Verlag.

Norberg, Arthur L. 2005. *Computers and Commerce: A Study of Technology and Management at Eckert-Mauchly Computer Company, Engineering Research Associates, and Remington Rand, 1946–1957*. Cambridge: MIT Press.

Pressey, Sidney L. 1926. "A Simple Apparatus which Gives Tests and Scores—and Teaches." *School and Society* 23 (586): 668–72.

Schestakow, Aleksandr Ivanovič, ed. 1965. *Programmiertes Lernen und Lehrmaschinen*. Berlin: Berlin Verlag.

Schirm, Rolf W. 1964. "Programmierte Unterweisung in der westdeutschen Industrie." In *Programmierter Unterricht und Lehrmaschinen: Bericht Internationale Konferenz Berlin*, edited by Armand Bianchérie, Ernst R. Hilgard, Harry M. B. Hurwitz, P. Kenneth Komoski, Gerald A. Randell, Halmuth Schaefer, and Walter Schultze, 126–33. Berlin: Pädagogische Arbeitsstelle Berlin.

Schmidt, Hermann. 1941. "Regelungstechnik: Die technische Aufgabe und ihre wirtschaftliche, sozialpolitische und kulturpolitische Auswirkung." *Zeitschrift des Vereins Deutscher Ingenieure* 85 (4): 81–88.

Skinner, Burrhus Frederic. 1958. "Teaching Machines: From the Experimental Study of Learning Come Devices Which Arrange Optimal Conditions for Self-Instruction." *Science* 128 (3330): 969–77.

———. 1983. *A Matter of Consequences*. New York: Knopf.

Texas Instruments. 1972. *Das TTL-Kochbuch: Deutschsprachige TTL-Applikationen*. Freising: Texas Instruments Deutschland GmbH Applikationslabor.

Thomas, Christina. 2006. "Überblick zur historischen Entwicklung von computerunterstützten Lehr- und Lernsystemen." Bachelor thesis, Technische Universität Dresden.

Vogt, Hans-Heinrich. 1966. *Der Nürnberger Trichter: Lernmaschinen für ihr Kind?* Stuttgart: Kosmos.

Watters, Audrey. 2021. *Teaching Machines: The History of Personalized Learning*. Cambridge: MIT Press.

Zöller, Wolfgang. 1975. *Planspiele in der Ausbildung: Darstellung, Ziele, Kritik, Weiterentwicklung*. Frankfurt am Main: Deutsch.

Zuther, Friedrich. 1996. *Die Aufhebung der Lehrautomatenentwicklung im Zuge der Entwicklung der Arbeitsplatzrechner: Monographien zur Kybernetik Series, Volume 1*. Aachen: Shaker.

BLACK BOX

NON-TRIVIAL MACHINE

MECHANIZATION

EPISTEMOLOGY

The Ashby Box: A Contextualization and Speculative Remake

Thomas Fischer and Andrei Cretu

Alan Turing and W. Ross Ashby drew on mechanization to probe the limits of two principal avenues to knowledge: deductive reasoning and experience-based induction. Turing proposed the Turing machine to ascertain the scope of the formally determinable, while Ashby built the Ashby Box to demonstrate the limits of experience-based induction. Whereas the Turing machine, a hypothetical thought experiment, was not meant to be built, the Ashby Box, a physical implementation of a black box, was not meant to be unriddled, or "whitened." Yet, just as Turing machines have been implemented, we set out to construct a device whose outward behavior matches that of the Ashby Box. In this

 chapter, we present the results of this effort. To contextualize this work, we trace a lineage of hardware and hypothetical machines, which arose from frictions between the predictability that makes life survivable and the unpredictability that makes life interesting. This lineage comprises four-terminal networks, the Turing machine, the Enigma cipher machine, the homeostat, the black box, the Ashby Box, and the non-trivial machine.

Prologue

In the early summer of 1935, a few weeks before his 23rd birthday, Alan Turing pondered one of the three questions David Hilbert had raised in 1928 on the limits of mathematics (Hilbert and Ackermann [1928] 1950, 112–24; Hodges 2014, 117). Two of these questions had already been answered by Kurt Gödel in the meantime, one about the completeness and the other about the consistency of mathematics—while one question remained concerning decidability, known as the decision problem (*Entscheidungsproblem*). Turing phrased it roughly like this: "Is there a 'general mechanical process' for telling whether any given formula is provable?" (Copeland 2017, 59). This phrasing bears the signature of the Cambridge University lecturer Max Newman, who had recently introduced Hilbert's decision problem in a lecture course on the foundations of mathematics, which Turing had attended (Grattan-Guinness 2013, 54–55). Newman had used the word "mechanical" whereas Hilbert had used the word "formal" (Hodges 2012, 93; Price 2021, 39). Turing, taking Newman's phrasing literally—as he was prone to (Hodges 2012, 123, 293)—dreamt of machines as he pondered the question. Catching his breath during a long-distance run on

that early summer's day, he conceived of the Turing machine—a
hypothetical mechanism with which he showed that computable and non-computable functions cannot be distinguished by
formal, that is, mechanical means (Turing 1937, 259).

The conflation of the formal with the mechanical was not new,
dating back to at least the 17th century when Gottfried Wilhelm
Leibniz sought to reduce formal logic to mechanics (Couturat 1901,
115). Much unlike Turing, however, Leibniz also aimed to reconcile
the formal and the spiritual. In particular, Leibniz sought to
square the existence of evil and suffering in the world with divine
benevolence, arriving at the notion that ours is the best of all possible worlds God could have created (Schneider 2002, 15). Now,
at the dawn of the electronic era, Turing pondered the limits of
mathematics rather than divine creation. In doing so, he helped
lay the foundations of the digital computer and thus, incidentally,
accelerated the formalization and mechanization of society.
George Dyson nonetheless suggests that regardless of how far
computers develop, computable and non-computable functions
keep the human condition in a fundamental balance:

> Turing proved that within any formal (or mechanical) system,
> ... there is no definite method to distinguish computable
> from noncomputable functions in advance. That's the bad
> news. The good news is that, as Leibniz suggested, we
> appear to live in the best of all possible worlds, where the
> computable functions make life predictable enough to be
> survivable, while the noncomputable functions make life
> (and mathematical truth) unpredictable enough to remain
> interesting, no matter how far computers continue to
> advance. (Dyson 2011, 50)

Soon, the will to survive demanded the defeat of Nazi Germany.
Attention had to be turned away from machines of abstract
philosophy and instead drawn to the concrete machinery of
warfare. The German military deployed electromechanical
rotor cipher machines to scramble plain text into seemingly

 random sequences of characters for radio transmission, and then to unscramble what was received back into plain text. Instrumental to the Allied victory, and with the benefit of pre-war achievements by Polish cryptanalysts, code-breakers at the UK Government Code and Cypher School at Bletchley Park devised and mechanized procedures to help turn intercepted German cipher traffic into readable German at an industrial scale. Alan Turing and Max Newman contributed these procedures for traffic enciphered with the Enigma machine family, and for traffic enciphered with the Lorenz machine family, respectively (Christensen 2007; Hodges 2014; Price 2021).

As a catalyst for the development of the digital computer, the automation of cryptanalysis at Bletchley Park also contributed to the mechanization of society. Thus, the balance between the predictably computable and the interestingly non-computable described so optimistically by Dyson was upset further in favor of mechanization—although Cassandra-like warnings against the threats of mechanization had long been written on the walls. Even before the digital computer entered the picture, George Orwell ([1937] 2021, 138) lamented "mechanization, rationalization, modernization" and Max Weber observed parallels between the mechanization of industry and the proliferation of bureaucratic forms of organization:

> The decisive reason for the advance of bureaucratic organization has always been its purely technical superiority over any other form of organization. The fully developed bureaucratic apparatus compares with other organizations exactly as does the machine with the non-mechanical modes of production. (Weber 1978, 973–74)

Later, with the digital computer in the picture, both as a product and as an instrument of technical formalization, the tendency toward the mechanization of society was bound to enter a positive feedback loop:

Instead of functioning actively as an autonomous personality, man will become a passive, purposeless, machine-conditioned animal whose proper functions, as technicians now interpret man's role, will either be fed into the machine or strictly limited and controlled for the benefit of de-personalized, collective organizations. (Mumford 1967, 3)

A backlash against the mechanization of society was forming—in particular within cybernetics (Wiener [1948] 1961, 27–28; 1989, 162) and, later, the broader 1960s counterculture (Turner 2006). As a part of this backlash, cybernetician Heinz von Foerster formulated his own take on decidability—not with Turing's interest in mechanistic determinability in mind, but with an interest in the autonomy humans enjoy in the *absence* of mechanistic determinability. He distinguishes between decidable questions, such as "is the number 3,396,714 divisible by 2?" and undecidable questions, like "the question about the origin of the universe" (von Foerster 2003, 291–92), as follows:

> Only those questions that are in principle undecidable, *we* can decide. ... decidable questions are already decided by the choice of the framework in which they are asked, and by the choice of the rules used to connect what we label "the question" with what we take for an "answer." ... we are under no compulsion, not even under that of logic, when we decide on in principle undecidable questions. There is no external necessity that forces us to answer such questions one way or another. We are free! The compliment to necessity is not chance, it is choice! *We can choose who we wish to become when we have decided on an in principle undecidable question.* (Von Foerster 2003, 293)

To illustrate this principle, von Foerster introduced two hypothetical devices, named the trivial machine (TM) and the non-trivial machine (NTM) (von Foerster 2003, 309–13; Glanville 2003, 98–101; Fischer 2013a, 1381–82). Both machines have input as well as output interfaces, but different internal configurations.

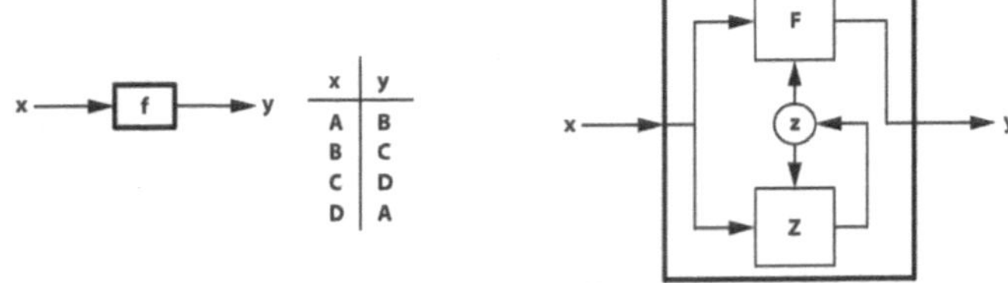

[Fig. 1] Trivial machine (left) and non-trivial machine (right). Redrawn from von Foerster (2003, 310–11).

The differences between these internal configurations have epistemic consequences for external onlookers who try to construct mental models of the machines' behaviors, i.e., observers aiming to "whiten" "black boxes" in Glanville's terms (1982). The TM is characterized by fixed associations between possible inputs and outputs. This allows an observer, after a period of monitoring the machine's input–output translations, to establish an assignment table, such as the one shown on the left of figure 1, and, based on that, predict the machine's output responses to given inputs, regardless of how long the machine has been in operation.

The NTM, by contrast, contains means to memorize an internal machine state (labeled z on the right of fig. 1), which, by definition, remains concealed from external observation. Each input–output translation changes this internal state, and each output is co-determined by both the input and the internal state. The NTM's input–output relationships thus depend on its history of input–output translations, with each translation effectively turning it into a different machine. The combinatorial space between possible inputs and possible internal states can result in vast numbers of input–output relationships that render the machine effectively unpredictable from an observer's perspective (von Foerster 2003, 74, 312; Krippendorff 2009b, 320–21).

This characteristic, achievable by mechanistic means, renders the NTM a twofold reflection of the human condition. On the one hand, its structure and the quality of behavior that arises 169 from it resemble those of our own. We humans perceive, act, and encompass internal states. Our internal states change through our perceptions and actions, and co-determine our actions, rendering us difficult to predict. In this sense, the NTM emblematizes our indeterminable selves.[1] On the other hand, with the vastness of its combinatorial possibilities exceeding human analytical capabilities, the NTM emblematizes the indeterminable objects of inquiry that permeate our experience.

Our inevitable failure to predict non-trivial systems can be a desirable and delightful source of magic and wonder (Glanville 2003; von Foerster 2003, 325–38), and may be harnessed in creative processes (Fischer 2013b). Unpredictability, creativity, and spontaneous novelty are unwelcome, however, where predictability is expected. Von Foerster (2003, 311) exemplifies this with a story of a child who, when asked "how much is 2 times 3?" responds "green" and is promptly reprimanded for this answer. With the juxtaposition of his two machines, von Foerster challenges the general expectation of, and adherence to, predictable behavior at the social level. In particular, he challenges the educational practice of "trivializing" young people:

> The majority of our established educational efforts is directed toward the trivialization of our children. I use the term "trivialization" exactly as used in automata theory, where a trivial machine is characterized by its fixed input–output relation, while in a non-trivial machine (Turing machine) the output is determined by the input *and* its internal state. Since our educational system is geared to generate predictable citizens, its aim is to amputate the bothersome internal states which generate unpredictability and novelty. This is most clearly demonstrated by our method of examination in which only questions are asked for which the

---

1   Shannon (1993), conversely, proposes a "mind reading (?)" machine capable of predicting binary human choices.

answers are known (or defined), and are to be memorized by the student. ...

Would it not be fascinating to think of an educational system that de-trivializes its students by teaching them to ask ... questions for which the answers are unknown? (Von Foerster 2003, 196)

At first glance, Turing delineating the decidability of computable functions and von Foerster recognizing undecidability as a force resisting trivialization appear to have little more in common than either's body of work being illustrated with a hypothetical machine. On closer examination, however, further connections come into view. The machines described in both cases have states that co-determine, and are determined by, their operations, allowing either of them to affect its own behavior via circularly-causal feedback.[2] The Turing machine and NTM furthermore demonstrate the limits of two avenues to knowledge: formal deduction and experience-based induction, respectively. Both machines, moreover, appear to share a common lineage, connected via devices built by the British cybernetician W. Ross Ashby. These devices and the NTM resemble the Enigma cipher machine to varying degrees (Tessmann 2008, 54–55; Fischer 2013a; 2018, 401–07). A key device in this lineage and a direct precursor to the NTM is the Ashby Box, designed and built by W. Ross Ashby in the 1960s. In the following sections, we present the results of our speculative effort to remake this device. We contextualize this effort amidst the lineage of related devices, highlighting the Ashby Box as a demonstration of epistemic limits and as both a product and a source of frictions between reliable predictability and unpredictable spontaneity (Fischer 2010, 611).

2   Recognizing this similarity, von Foerster (2003, 196) describes the NTM as an instance of the Turing machine.

An Elementary Object of Inquiry

On Saturday, January 20, 1951, fifteen and a half years after Turing conceived of the Turing machine during a long-distance run, the British psychiatrist and cybernetician W. Ross Ashby hosted an informal meeting with MIT professor Norbert Wiener at the Burden Neurological Institute in Bristol (Ashby 1951, 3075). Wiener, 56 years old at the time, and nine years Ashby's senior, was visiting from Paris, where he had arrived a month earlier on a Fulbright Teaching Fellowship (Conway and Siegelman 2005, 211), and where both Wiener and Ashby had attended a conference a few days earlier (Carpenter 2018).

At the time, both Ashby and Wiener had already made foundational contributions to their emerging discipline. Wiener had published the first edition of his book *Cybernetics* (Wiener [1948] 1961), the title of which was soon adopted as the name of the new field. Ashby had finished work on his homeostat (Ashby 1948, 2431–32; 1954b), a device embodying his understanding of the mammalian brain's ability "to adapt by internal re-organization" and "work out an essential part of its own wiring" (Ashby 1949, 77). In principle, the homeostat consisted of an arbitrary number of electrically interconnected units. Ashby built a homeostat out of four such units using, as he describes (Ashby 1948, 2431), Royal Air Force "bomb control switch gear kits."[3]

The homeostat incorporated two nested feedback loops. The inner loop maintained stability between four continuous variables embodied in the four units' top-mounted, liquid-based, manually and electromagnetically moveable potentiometers. Disturbances introduced to any of the four potentiometers were compensated by those of the remaining units to maintain stable overall averages. When the homeostat found an overall

---

3   Apparently referring to the appropriation of the 16 toggle switches from a Type F 5D/656 16-way bomb selector control panel of an Avro Lancaster heavy bomber.

 equilibrium alignment of its potentiometers—each with a tendency toward its midpoint—the potentiometers actively resisted attempts at displacing them. The outer loop achieved ultra-stability through spontaneous self-reconfiguration whenever the homeostat failed to reach a tenable overall equilibrium. In such situations, the four units would search randomly for a tenable alternative out of sets of available resistors within, and possible interconnections between them.

The homeostat's capability to self-reconfigure open-endedly in response to its inputs and internal states was exceedingly rare among man-made devices at the time, if not unprecedented (Pickering 2002, 417). The components that enabled the four homeostat units to perform their searches for ultra-stability were stepper-motor-driven rotary switches called uniselectors. Already widely used to automate telephone exchanges (Strowger 1891), uniselectors had also been adopted in a variety of control and data-processing applications in the electromechanical era for their capability to perform controlled variations of electrical interconnections. They had been used, to name a few examples: in Japanese polyalphabetic cipher machines designated by US cryptanalysts as CORAL and JADE (Freeman et al. 2003); in totalizators—machines for managing sports betting—(Swade 2019, 45); and in the Colossus computer built at Bletchley Park to accelerate the cryptanalysis of the German Lorenz cipher (Flowers 2006, 95–97), based on an automation scheme envisioned by Max Newman (Price 2021, 100; Newman 2006).

Around 15 people attended the 1951 meeting in Bristol, hand-picked mainly from Bristol University and Oxford University. The discussions, however, remained almost entirely between Wiener, Ashby, and Ashby's colleague and fellow cybernetician Grey Walter. Ashby, who would in time emerge as "the next leader of cybernetics theory after Wiener" (Conway and Siegelman 2005, 278), was delighted with Wiener's approval of his work. Wiener (1989, 38) would later praise Ashby's "brilliant idea of the unpurposeful random mechanism which seeks for its own purpose through a process of learning" as "one of the great philo- sophical contributions of the present day."

Among the matters discussed in Bristol that day, one stood out to Ashby. It was what Wiener called the "problem of the black box" (Ashby 1951, 3076). In the introduction of the second edition of *Cybernetics*, Wiener described this problem as follows:

> I shall understand by a black box a piece of apparatus, such as four-terminal networks with two input and two output terminals, which performs a definite operation on the present and past of the input potential, but for which we do not necessarily have any information of the structure by which this operation is performed. On the other hand, a white box will be a similar network in which we have built in the relation between input and output potentials in accordance with a definite structural plan for securing a previously determined input–output relation. (Wiener [1948] 1961, xi)

The concept of the black box developed circuitously with multiple adoptions and varying interpretations of the term (Petrick 2020). According to McCulloch, Wiener encountered a variant of the black box problem at a meeting both he and McCulloch attended on January 6 and 7, 1945,[4] at the Institute of Advanced Study at Princeton University:

> Lorente de Nó and I, as physiologists, were asked to consider the second of two hypothetical black boxes that the allies had liberated from the Germans. No one knew what they were supposed to do or how they were to do it. The first box had been opened and exploded. Both had inputs and outputs, so labelled. The question was phrased unforgettably: "This is the enemy's machine. You always have to

---

4   Echoing Wiener ([1948] 1961, xi), McCulloch misdates this meeting as
     occurring in the winter of 1943–44. Written correspondence between
     meeting participants, however, shows this to be an error (Heims 1993, 294,
     note 44; von Hilgers 2011, 55, note 13).

find out what it does and how it does it. What shall we do?" (McCulloch 1989, 40)

McCulloch continues with an account of Wiener, John von Neumann, and others engaging in a spirited exchange on how best to proceed when facing such a device. Von Hilgers (2010, 150; 2011, 52, 55–56) notes that the phrase "black box" itself was probably not used explicitly at the meeting, but observes that "the contours of a black box" had clearly been present.

The term "black box" likely originated in German-speaking Central Europe, where the concept of four-terminal networks was formalized before World War II to address the telecommunications engineering challenge of diagnosing unknown or inaccessible circuitry (Breisig 1921; Feldtkeller 1937). Feldtkeller describes this concept as "a closed box with four terminals" (*ein verschlossener Kasten mit 4 Polen*) and unknown contents—*"der Inhalt des Kastens [ist] in Einzelheiten unbekannt"* (Feldtkeller 1937, 1). With his reference to a "box," Feldtkeller emphasizes the concealment of its inner workings, rather than suggesting a physical scale. He notes:

> The "box" may have grotesque dimensions—if, for example, our "four-terminal network" shall reach all the way from the input terminals of a broadcast antenna to the output terminals of a remote receiver antenna. (Feldtkeller 1937, 1)[5]

Ashby's interest in black box theory, by contrast, had little to do with the diagnosis and remediation of engineering nuisances. Instead of technical troubleshooting, he was interested in the probing of unknown circuitry as a quintessential exemplar of how we come to know (Glanville 2007). Ashby explains:

> In our daily lives we are confronted at every turn with systems whose internal mechanisms are not fully open

5   Authors' translations.

to inspection, and which must be treated by the methods appropriate to the Black Box. (Ashby 1957, 86)

Pondering what an observer (or experimenter) does when probing a black box, he asked:

> "How should an experimenter proceed when faced with a Black Box?"

> "What properties of the Black Box's content are discoverable and what are fundamentally not discoverable?"

> "What methods should be used if the Box is to be investigated efficiently?"

> (Ashby 1957, 86–87)

In short, Ashby was interested in the black box as an elementary object of epistemic inquiry.

Ashby's Black Box

To develop a theory of inquiry into black boxes, Ashby needed a model object in which to inquire, i.e., an actual black box to configure and probe. Addressing this need, Ashby built a hardware device, which he named the "black box." Completed in 1954, it consisted of two metal boxes and a plugboard (see the center of fig. 2). It accepted inputs via four toggle switches and produced outputs via four lamps. On the side of one of the two boxes, a crank protruded from an internal rotational switch, crafted by Ashby himself (Ashby 1954a, 4951). Four vanes radiating from the switch's rotating shaft "like a windmill" acted as contacts, which, with each full turn of the crank, generated a four-step sequence that changed the machine's state. The first step of the sequence transferred the machine's output from the output register to its memory. The second step cleared the output register. The third step set the output register to a new value based on the wiring set up on the plugboard, incorporating, in some operator-defined way, the machine's input and the contents of its memory. The fourth step, finally, cleared the machine's memory. Both the memory and the output register were implemented with latching relays.

Notably, the main features of the black box matched those of the Enigma cipher machine (see the left of fig. 2). Its input switches and output lamps, its external plugboard, and its state transitions based on rotational switching all had corresponding features in the Enigma machine,[6] suggesting that the Enigma machine may have had a design influence on the black box (Fischer 2012, 683; 2013a, 1376). While there is no conclusive evidence to confirm this, circumstances indicate that this is a possibility. In late 1946, Ashby exchanged letters with the former Enigma code-breaker Turing. In their correspondence, Ashby and Turing discussed possible uses of a new digital computer Turing was helping to develop at the National Physical Laboratory at the time: the Automatic Computing Engine, or ACE (Copeland 2006, 108). Ashby inquired as to whether the ACE could be used to "model the action of the brain," which Turing, sharing similar interests (Greif 2018), affirmed enthusiastically (Turing 1946; Hodges 2014, 452–53). Turing, nearly nine years Ashby's junior, wrote to Ashby that the ACE was analogous to the Turing machine. Ashby, in turn, would later categorize the Turing machine as a "finite-state transducer" (Ashby 1954a, 5042)—a categorization that likewise applies to his black box. Ultimately, despite Turing's assurances, Ashby opted against using the ACE and, instead, implemented his theories of brain activity electromechanically in what would become the homeostat (Vater 2020, 336).

Between 1949 and Turing's death in 1954, Ashby and Turing met regularly as members of the Ratio Club, a circle of British cyberneticians (Husbands and Holland 2008; Hodges 2014, 518).

---

6   The variable state of the Enigma machine (specifically, the selection, configuration, and rotational positions of its rotors) is not influenced by its output. Instead, its state iterates, with some degree of irregularity, with each input–output translation.

[Fig. 2] Enigma Machine (left), Ashby's black box (center), and the Ashby Box (right). Sources left to right: Private Collection/Photo © Christie's Images/Bridgeman Images. Courtesy of the Estate of W. Ross Ashby and the Ross Ashby Digital Archive, http://www.rossashby.info. Jamie Hutchinson, University of Illinois, reproduced with permission.

While the Official Secrets Act prevented Turing from divulging his war-time cryptanalytical insights, he was free to talk about the working principles of the Enigma machine, which had been known to the public since its initial patenting in 1918. It is thus conceivable that the Enigma machine influenced Ashby's design of the black box via Turing. Consistent with this scenario, several facets of the Enigma machine became recurring themes in Ashby's work after he had made contact with Turing. These include: immense combinatorial variety (Hodges 2014, 210–24; Ashby [1964] 1991; Fischer 2018, 793–96), internal state transitions in electromechanical devices with the use of rotating switches, and, also inspired by Wiener, the whitening of black boxes from external vantage points.

Ashby used the black box as a teaching aid during his tenure at von Foerster's Biological Computer Laboratory (BCL) at the University of Illinois in the 1960s. A handout survives from an undergraduate course Ashby taught during that period, titled "EE473 Fundamentals of Cybernetics." The five-page document introduces the working principles of the black box, followed by an assignment to specify and program a set of behaviors for the device. Ashby's students were to accomplish this in several steps: first by describing the intended behavior in plain English, then in the form of truth tables, later as four two-terminal circuits, and, finally, as a wiring setup on the machine's plugboard. Unfortunately, the purpose of the exercise does not emanate from the handout. It may have been to explicate an insight Ashby had gained when interacting with the black box soon after its completion in 1954. Ashby (1954a, 4953) wanted to find out if the device could be controlled. Specifically, he wanted to know to what extent an operator could attain intended output states by manipulating the device's inputs and plugboard configuration. This, it turned out, varied considerably. In many instances, control over the device's output was limited or even impossible, and the operator had to figure out what was possible at each instance.

To attain intended states, it was necessary to anticipate how the black box would respond to its inputs and plugboard configuration. The capacity to do so had to be established by observing the device's behavior over a period of time, establishing a general pattern based on specific instances. In essence, it required inductive reasoning. The black box demonstrated that the reliability of inductive reasoning is limited if the system in question cannot be grasped in full. The defining characteristic of the black box, in this sense, was that some portion of it could not be inspected, to the effect that some variables significant to its behavior were obscured. It is this partial observability, Ashby reasoned, that allows systems to appear miraculous to external observers—much like conjuring appears miraculous to spectators who are not aware of the entirety of the conjurer's stagecraft (Ashby 1951, 3105; 1954a, 4951–53; 1956, 114). The outcomes of Ashby's classroom exercise are unknown. His subsequent implementation of a radically simplified successor device suggests, however, that a desire emerged in this context for a more straightforward demonstration object.

The Ashby Box

The successor to Ashby's black box was more compact and more straightforward to operate than its predecessor, yet it preserved its key principles. Contained in a single aluminum box and shown on the right in figure 2, it is commonly referred to as the "Ashby Box." Notwithstanding its early electromechanical vintage, it is arguably among the most minimal and refined cybernetic demonstration devices.[7] Its input interface consists of two toggle switches, each of which can be in an up or a down position, allowing four possible input patterns. Its output interface consists of two lamps, each of which can be either on or off, allowing four possible output patterns. Toggling either switch causes the device to change the on/off pattern of its output lamps in a highly unpredictable way.[8] Its inner workings, albeit mechanically deterministic, entail vast combinatorial possibilities that exceed human capabilities for systematic exploration and analysis. This is reflected in von Foerster's accounts of perplexed BCL students trying to determine the device's transfer function:

> W. Ross Ashby, who worked with me at the Biological Computer Laboratory, built a little machine with 4 outputs, 4 inputs, and 4 inner states, and gave this machine to the graduate students, who wanted to work with him. He told them, they were to figure out for him how this machine worked, he'd be back in the morning. Now, I was a night person, I've always gotten to the lab only around noon and then gone home around 1, 2, or 3 in the morning. So I saw these poor creatures sitting and working and writing up tables and I told them: "Forget it! You can't figure it out!"— "No, no, I've almost got it already!" At six A.M. the next morning they were still sitting there, pale and green. The next day Ross Ashby said to them: "Forget it! I'll tell you how

7   A family of circuits designed later at the BCL by Ricardo Uribe featuring double-pole, double-throw switches (Uribe 1991; Kauffman 1996, 196) arguably surpasses the Ashby Box in these qualities.
8   The first author interacted with the Ashby Box during demonstrations by Ricardo Uribe in Champaign-Urbana, Illinois in 2008.

many possibilities you have: 10^{126}." So then they relaxed. (Von Foerster 2003, 312)[9]

The label it bears, dating back to the BCL years, designates the device as "Ashby's Elementary NTM." Likely applied by von Foerster, this label has intriguing implications regarding the lineage and purpose of the device. It suggests that the Ashby Box inspired von Foerster's NTM. It furthermore suggests that Ashby and von Foerster jointly considered the reduction and theoretical description of non-triviality. In any case, it implies that von Foerster's NTM and the Ashby Box share a common root, with the NTM likely having been inspired by the Ashby Box and its predecessor, the black box, and hence, possibly, by the Enigma machine (Fischer 2013a).

Following Ashby's retirement in 1970, the device remained in the BCL inventory until the lab's dissolution in the mid-1970s, after which Ricardo Uribe took custody of the device until his death in 2019.[10] Over the years, the owners and custodians of the Ashby Box have concealed its internal mechanism from curious eyes. What is generally known about the device was reported by individuals who experienced it as hands-on experimenters or spectators (von Foerster 2003, 312; 2014, 24–25; Krippendorff 2009a, 191). Its internals are not meant to be known and, apart from audible rumblings that give away its electromechanical nature during state changes, they remain a mystery to this day.

Müggenburg (2016, 79–80) notes that the value of the Ashby Box is predicated on the concealment of its innards in two ways: on the one hand, it veils the particularities of its implementation, emphasizing its abstract qualities, thereby allowing it to stand

---

9   In a verbal account of this episode, von Foerster later added: "if you have a path-dependent system, … you can't analyze it. It's absolutely impossible. The two steps, two lamps, two switches, it's … you can't crack the code of that machine" (Müggenburg and Pias 2013, 61).

10   Today, the Ashby Box is kept in the University of Illinois Archives along with Uribe's papers under Record Series 11/6/40.

in for any object of inquiry. On the other hand, it gives rise to
the magic and wonder that make its performance epistemically
productive. This latter quality reflects von Foerster's lifelong
fascination with magic. An accomplished stage magician since
his childhood, von Foerster worked out, refined, performed, and
protected the secrecy of magic tricks (Dotzler 1996; von Foerster
2003, 325–38; Glanville 2003, 98–101; Müggenburg 2016). Uribe's
refusal to allow insights into the Ashby Box during his demonstrations of the device likewise reflect the magician's refusal
to divulge magic tricks to non-magicians.[11] According to Uribe,
nobody but himself was allowed to open the Ashby Box, which he
did from time to time when it required "a drop of oil."[12]

Thus, hypothetical and physical mechanization was deployed to
probe the limits of two principal avenues to knowledge: deductive
reasoning and experience-based induction. Turing had proposed
a hypothetical machine to ascertain the limits of the formally
provable. Ashby, then, implemented an experimental mechanism
to explore the limits of what can be ascertained through experience and induction. Unlike other technical devices such as type-
writers and electric kettles, the purpose of the Ashby Box was not
to bring about reliably predictable, utilitarian change, but rather
to demonstrate the qualities of epistemic objects. Unlike other
abstract conjectures, such as Schrödinger's cat and the Turing
machine, the Ashby Box was no mere mental construct, but
rather an actual technical mechanism. It was a thought experiment among mechanical devices, and a mechanical device among
thought experiments.

As a thought experiment, the Turing machine was not meant
to be built. As a physical implementation of a black box, the
Ashby Box, in turn, was not meant to be unriddled. Yet, as Turing

11   Or, analogously, the cryptographer's duty to conceal private encryption
      keys.
12   Uribe's 2008 words. Personal communication with the first author, cited
      from memory.

182 machines have been implemented in hardware (Davey 2021) and software emulation (Fischer 2018, 312–14), so we set out to speculatively remake the Ashby Box. Without insights into its inner workings and without performing a detailed analysis of its behavior, we speculated how a generally comparable equivalent of the original device might be implemented using components that were common at the time of its implementation and featured in other works of its designer. In doing so, we arrived at and built two speculative remakes of the device—enclosed and open, respectively—which we describe in the following paragraphs. Readers enamored with the Ashby Box and wishing to avoid any possible disenchantment may want to skip the remainder of this section.

At any time, a machine with a 2-bit input and a 2-bit output, be it trivial or non-trivial, behaves according to one of $4^4 = 256$ transfer functions—i.e., one of 256 possible mappings of its four possible input patterns to its four possible output patterns (von Foerster 2003, 312). While these mappings remain unvaried in TMs, they vary in NTMs with each operation. The current state of an NTM with a 2-bit input and a 2-bit output thus represents the presently active selection out of 256 possible transfer functions. Knowledge of the number of an NTM's possible internal states is, accordingly, a key to determining its behavior. Von Foerster's (2003, 312) disclosure that the combinatorial variety of the Ashby Box is 10^{126} offers a clue in this regard, raising the question: how many internal states are needed for a machine with a 2-bit input and a 2-bit output to reach a combinatorial variety of 10^{126}? The combinatorial variety of non-trivial machines grows exponentially with the number of internal states. In a 2-bit input and 2-bit output NTM with a combinatorial variety of 10^{126}, the number of required internal states is $\log_{256} 10^{126}$. Assuming 10^{126} to be a ballpark figure, this would be the natural number to which 256 is to be raised to best

Sw1S1	0	0	1	1
Sw2S1	0	1	0	1
f_0	00	00	00	00
f_1	00	00	00	01
f_2	00	00	00	10
f_3	00	00	00	11
f_4	00	00	00	00
f_5	00	00	01	01
f_6	00	00	01	10
$f_{...}$	...	...	...	...
f_{248}	11	11	10	00
f_{249}	11	11	10	01
f_{250}	11	11	10	10
f_{251}	11	11	10	11
f_{252}	11	11	11	00
f_{253}	11	11	11	01
f_{254}	11	11	11	10
f_{255}	11	11	11	11

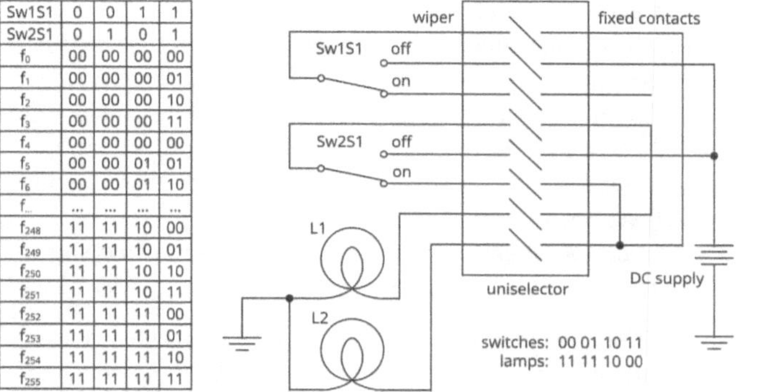

[Fig. 3] Left: Truth table of possible transfer functions of the Ashby Box. Right: Wiring of a column of fixed contacts on an 8-bank uniselector corresponding to f_{248}.

approximate 10^{126}. Accordingly,[13] the number of internal states required is 52:

$$256^{51} = 6.61099568 \times 10^{122}$$
$$256^{52} = 1.69230328 \times 10^{125}$$
$$256^{53} = 4.33229639 \times 10^{127}$$

Interestingly, 52 happens to be the number of switching positions on a type of rotary uniselector that was widely used in electromechanical telephone exchanges. A variation of a yet more common 26-position uniselector type (James 1964, 13), it features a rotor with two diametrically opposed wiper assemblies whose two sets of eight moving contacts scan alternate (odd and even) banks of fixed contacts during each half rotation, resulting in a 52-way switch (see the right of fig. 5).[14] This might have allowed implementing 52 internal states by connecting the two input switches and the two output lamps of the Ashby Box to the

---

13   python3 -c "import math; print(round(math.log(10**126, 256)))"
14   The 26 and 52 switching positions appear to be vestiges from uniselector
      applications to cryptographic systems based on 26-letter alphabets (Turing
      2001, 3).

 contacts of the rotor, and wiring random transfer functions on
each of the 52 available contact columns by connecting various
combinations of contacts (Cretu 2020, 2077). In such a configuration, the uniselector's rotor position constitutes the device's
internal state, co-determining its current transfer function. Its
latching stepwise motion ensures the retention of its state until
the next state transition is initiated—also during power supply
interruptions. A schematic description of this approach is shown
in figure 3.

The table on the left of figure 3 shows some of the 256 possible
transfer functions of the Ashby Box with its 4-bit input and 4-bit
output. Its four columns of values correspond to the four input
conditions listed in the first two table rows: 0;0, 0;1, 1;0, and 1;1.
Each double-digit value in the table gives the corresponding
output. In state f_{248}, for example, the input 0;0 gives the output
11, the input 0;1 gives the output 11, the input 1;0 gives the output
10, and the input 1;1 gives the output 00. Out of the possible 256
transfer functions indicated on the left of figure 3, we chose
26 and 52 at random, and implemented them on the 26 and 52
positions of two uniselectors, respectively, in a random order.[15]

The input switches of the Ashby Box perform two functions.
Besides delivering the electrical on/off inputs, they also cause the
Ashby Box to transition from its present state to the next every
time they are toggled. This corresponds to the way the input keys
of the Enigma machine not only opened and closed the electrical
circuits that illuminated the machine's output lamps, but also
caused the mechanical advancement of its rotors. To perform
both these functions, the switches must be double-pole switches.
We used the second sections of the two double-pole switches
(Sw1 and Sw2) to implement a pulse generator that triggers the
uniselector's stepper motor (Uni) every time either switch is

---

15   Our random assignment of transfer functions is comparable to Ashby's con-
      nection of resistors to the uniselectors of the homeostat based on a table of
      random numbers (Ashby 1954b, 103).

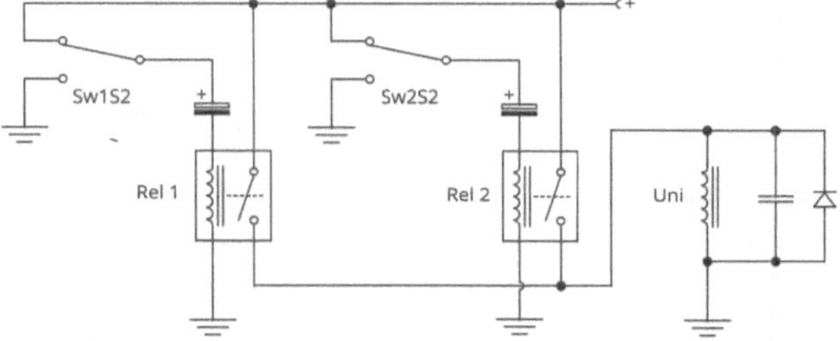

[Fig. 4] Pulse generator circuit to trigger the uniselector's stepper motor every time either switch is toggled.

[Fig. 5] Enigma rotor (left) and uniselector with the transfer functions wired (right).

[Fig. 6] Open remake of the Ashby Box based on a 2x8-pole, 52-position uniselector. The breadboard contains the pulse generator.

 toggled either way. Our circuit for this purpose is shown in figure 4.

Interactions with the resulting device(s) trace paths through the truth table shown on the left of figure 3, with the experimenter controlling the horizontal component of each step, and the vertical component then being determined, besides the random choice of transfer functions available in a given device, by the uniselector's wiring and current position. Every time an experimenter initiates a jump between the columns of the truth table by toggling either one or both of the input switches, the device also performs a jump to a different row. At each step in this process, the state of the two lamps is a function of the state of the two input switches. An experimenter interrogating the device and aiming to fully predict its behavior would need complete knowledge of its internal structure and current internal state— that is, almost 422 bits of information.[16] Without this knowledge, the device appears forever enigmatic, offering its observers no more than fleeting illusions of predictability (von Foerster 2014, 25).

Indeed, we experienced interactions with our remakes[17] as unpredictable, punctuated by fleeting illusions of predictability, and generally indistinguishable from interactions with the original Ashby Box. After their completion, some unexpected parallels between our remakes and the original became apparent. Externally visible screws used to mount the uniselector in the case of our enclosed remake[18] match the positions of corresponding screws in the case of the original Ashby Box.

16   Uncertainty about the current position of the uniselector's rotor, which amounts to $\log_{52} = 5.7$ bits plus the total "storage capacity" of the uniselector, which amounts to 52 rows of 8 bits from the table shown on the left in figure 3, i.e., 416 bits.

17   A video demonstration is available at https://youtu.be/ETtJfr6fZvQ?t=2843.

18   The enclosure shown in figure 7 was produced by Bud Industries, an Ohio-based manufacturer of enclosures established in 1928. Apparently, this was also the source of the enclosure of the original Ashby Box.

[Fig. 7] Enclosed remake of the Ashby Box based on an 8-pole, 26-position uniselector, opened (left), as well as closed and operating (right).

Furthermore, the lamps in both our remakes and in the original often illuminate transiently at the instant of internal state changes. In our remakes, this occurs while the uniselector's moving wipers are still touching the contact banks of their previous position, suggesting that a similar componentry and circuitry may be at play in the original.

Besides taking notice of some externally apparent similarities, we did not pursue these parallels any further. Adhering to both the fundamental epistemological condition the Ashby Box was designed to demonstrate, and the wishes of its designer and later custodians, we refrain from comparing (the innards of) our remakes against (those of) the original Ashby Box. We believe that the selection and sequence of transfer functions implemented in our remakes are unlikely to match those of the original, and therefore do not assume that our remakes can predict the exact behavior of the original. Experimenters can interact with either of our remakes *as if* it were the Ashby Box, but without gaining insight into the inner workings of, or being enabled to reliably predict, the original. To us, that is good enough. After all, the power of the black box is, as Glanville (2007, 195) notes, that we do not need to know what is in it.

Epilogue

In this chapter, we traced a lineage of hypothetical and hardware machines comprising four-terminal networks, the Turing machine, the Enigma cipher machine, the homeostat, the black box, the Ashby Box, and the non-trivial machine. Several meetings of leading minds gave rise to this lineage, including Turing and Wiener inspiring Ashby, and Ashby, in turn, inspiring von Foerster. Some machines in this lineage are input–output systems with internal states that are hidden from outside views. Their inputs and their internal states co-determine their outputs, while their internal states are affected by their outputs via circularly-causal feedback loops. In electromechanical hardware instances among these machines, state memory and state transitions tend to be based on rotational switching, in most cases using uniselectors. By varying their input–output transfer functions, the devices in this lineage turn into different devices with virtually every one of their input–output operations. They do so within potentially vast combinatorial spaces that far exceed human analytical capabilities. Ashby demonstrated this quality in a hardware device, the Ashby Box. Based on this, von Foerster presented the NTM—a hypothetical machine constituting a cornerstone of his critique of trivialization in social contexts.

Exemplifying the inscrutability of black boxes, the Ashby Box depends on the obscurity of its inner workings. Von Foerster's disclosure of its combinatorial variety and, based on that, our assumption that it may incorporate a uniselector allowed us to "whiten" the Ashby Box and implement two speculative remakes—one enclosed and one open. Despite revealing much of its technical functionality, the open remake is challenging to predict from an uninitiated experimenter's perspective. The enclosed remake, naturally, is even harder to predict. Neither remake offers reliable insights into the technical functionality of the original Ashby Box, nor do they enable the reliable prediction of the original's exact behavior. Yet, just as the original,

both remakes exhibit the unpredictability of non-trivial systems,
demonstrating the conditions from which wonder and magic can
arise even by entirely mechanistic means.

The Ashby Box and our remakes are technical objects that can, in
principle, be opened and analyzed. This, however, cannot belie
the ultimate inscrutability of the objects of inquiry these devices
represent. The black boxes surrounding us are not available for
complete inspection, exhaustive analysis, and entirely reliable
prediction. Not even trivial mechanisms operate as expected
indefinitely and may, at a minimum, require a "drop of oil" now
and then to remain trivial. Therefore, any "whitening" of a black
box is no more than a provisional conjecture, of whose accu-
racy there can be no ultimate confirmation, and the question of
whether it can be relied upon is, in the end, undecidable.

The lineage of devices with which we contextualized the Ashby
Box bridges technical, epistemological, and ethical concerns.
At the center of this lineage, Turing and Ashby deployed mechanization to delineate the limits of formal deduction and experience-based induction, respectively. On a broader scale, this
lineage departs from the analysis of four-terminal networks
and arrives at an appreciation of undecidable questions. It thus
progresses from the facilitation of technical troubleshooters to
the legitimization of creative troublemakers. Challenging mechanization and trivialization in epistemological and social contexts
with formal reasoning and a mechanical demonstration, Ashby
and von Foerster fought fire with fire. The blazes of this fight are
re-ignited time and again by frictions between the predictability
that makes life survivable and the unpredictability that makes life
interesting.

References

Ashby, W. Ross. 1948. "Journal 11." W. Ross Ashby Digital Archive. http://rossashby.
    info/journal/volume/11.html.
————.1949. "The Electronic Brain." *Radio-Electronics,* March 1949.

190   ———.1951. "Journal 13." W. Ross Ashby Digital Archive. http://rossashby.info/journal/volume/13.html.

———.1954a. "Journal 18." W. Ross Ashby Digital Archive. http://rossashby.info/journal/volume/18.html.

———.1954b. *Design for a Brain*, New York: Wiley.

———.1956. *An Introduction to Cybernetics*. London: Chapman and Hall.

———.1957. "Journal 20." W. Ross Ashby Digital Archive. http://rossashby.info/journal/volume/20.html.

———.(1964) 1991. "Introductory Remarks at Panel Discussion." In *Facets of Systems Science*, edited by George J. Klir, 507–10. New York: Plenum Press.

Breisig, Franz. 1921. "Über das Nebensprechen in Fernsprechkreisen." *Elektrotechnische Zeitschrift* 42 (34): 933–39.

Carpenter, Brian. 2018. "A Meeting that Missed its Mark: The Paris Conference of 1951." *Rutherford Journal* 5 (2018). http://rutherfordjournal.org/article050103.html.

Christensen, Chris. 2007. "Polish Mathematicians Finding Patterns in Enigma Messages." *Mathematics Magazine* 80 (4): 247–73.

Conway, Flo, and Jim Siegelman. 2005. *Dark Hero of the Information Age: In Search of Norbert Wiener, the Father of Cybernetics*. New York: Basic Books.

Copeland, Jack. 2006. "Colossus and the Rise of the Modern Computer." In *Colossus: The Secrets of Bletchley Park's Codebreaking Computers*, edited by Jack Copeland, 101–15. New York: Oxford University Press.

———.2017. "Hilbert and His Famous Problem." In *The Turing Guide*, edited by Jack Copeland, Jonathan Bowen, Mark Sprevak, and Robin Wilson, 57–65. Oxford: Oxford University Press.

Couturat, Louis. 1901. *La logique de Leibniz: D'après des documents inédits*. Paris: F. Alcan.

Cretu, Andrei. 2020. "Learning the Ashby Box: An Experiment in Second Order Cybernetic Modeling." *Kybernetes* 49 (8): 2073–90.

Davey, Mike. 2021. "A Turing Machine." Accessed January 12, 2023. https://aturingmachine.com.

Dyson, George. 2011. *Turing's Cathedral: The Origins of the Digital Universe*. New York: Pantheon Books.

Dotzler, Bernhard J. 1996. "Demons-magic-cybernetics: On the Introduction to Natural Magic as Told by Heinz von Foerster." *Systems Research* 13 (3): 245–50.

Feldtkeller, Richard. 1937. *Einführung in die Vierpoltheorie der elektrischen Nachrichtentechnik*. Leipzig: S. Hirzel.

Fischer, Thomas. 2010. "The Interdependence of Linear and Circular Causality in CAAD Research: A Unified Model." In *Proceedings of the 15th CAADRIA Conference*, edited by Bharat Dave, Andrew I-Kang Li, Ning Gu and Hyoung-June Park, A. I. Li, Ning Gu, and H.-J. Park, 609–18. Hong Kong: CAADRIA.

———.2012. "Design Enigma: A Typographical Metaphor for Enigmatic Processes, Including Designing." In *Proceedings of the 17th CAADRIA Conference*, edited by Thomas Fischer, Kaustuv De Biswas, Jeremy J. Ham, Ryusuke Naka, and Weixin Huang, 679–88. Hong Kong: CAADRIA.

———. 2013a. "Enigmatic Mechanisms in Defense of the Capability to Have New Ideas." *Kybernetes* 42 (9/10): 1374–86.

———. 2013b. "Circular Causality and Indeterminism in Machines for Design." *Frontiers of Architectural Research* 3 (4): 368–75.

———. 2018. "Kybernetik für Medienwissenschaftler." In *Medientechnisches Wissen Band 2: Informatik, Programmieren, Kybernetik,* edited by Stefan Höltgen, Thorsten Schöler, Johannes Maibaum, and Thomas Fischer. 273–433. Oldenburg: DeGruyter.

Flowers, Thomas H. 2006. "Colossus." In *Colossus: The Secrets of Bletchley Park's Codebreaking Computers,* edited by Jack Copeland, 91–100. New York: Oxford University Press.

Freeman, Wes, Geoff Sullivan, and Frode Weierud. 2003. "Purple Revealed: Simulation and Computer-Aided Cryptanalysis of Angooki Taipu B." *Cryptologia* 27 (1): 1–43.

Glanville, Ranulph. 1982. "Inside Every White Box There Are Two Black Boxes Trying to Get Out." *Behavioral Science* 27 (1): 1–11.

———. 2003. "Machines of Wonder and Elephants that Float Through Air: A Valedictory Understanding of Understanding Understanding." *Cybernetics & Human Knowing* 10 (3/4): 91–101.

———. 2007. "A (Cybernetic) Musing: Ashby and The Black Box." *Cybernetics & Human Knowing* 14 (2/3): 189–96.

Grattan-Guinness, Ivan. 2013. "The Mentor of Alan Turing: Max Newman (1897–1984) as a Logician." *The Mathematical Intelligencer* 35 (3): 54–63.

Greif, Hajo. 2018. "The Action of The Brain: Machine Models and Adaptive Functions in Turing and Ashby." In *Philosophy and Theory of Artificial Intelligence 2017,* edited by Vincent C. Müller, 24–35. Cham: Springer.

Heims, Steve Joshua. 1993. *Constructing a Social Science for Postwar America: The Cybernetics Group, 1946–1953.* Cambridge: MIT Press.

Hilbert, David, and Wilhelm Ackermann. (1928) 1950. *Principles of Mathematical Logic.* Providence: Chelsea Publishing.

Hodges, Andrew. 2014. *Alan Turing: The Enigma.* Princeton: Princeton University Press.

Husbands, Phil, and Owen Holland. 2008. "The Ratio Club: A Hub of British Cybernetics." In *The Mechanical Mind in History,* edited by Phil Husbands, Owen Holland, and Michael Wheeler, 91–148. Cambridge: MIT Press.

James, Virgil E., ed. 1964. *How to Use Rotary Stepping Switches.* Northlake: Automatic Electric.

Kauffman, Louis H. 1996. "Virtual Logic." *Systems Research* 13 (3): 293–310.

Krippendorff, Klaus. 2009a. "Ross Ashby's Information Theory: A Bit of History, Some Solutions to Problems, and What We Face Today." *International Journal of General Systems* 38 (2): 189–212.

———. 2009b. "Four (In)Determinabilities, Not One." In *Indeterminacy: The Mapped, the Navigable, and the Uncharted,* edited by Jose V. Ciprut, 315–44. Cambridge: MIT Press.

192 McCulloch, Warren S. 1989. "Recollections of the Many Sources of Cybernetics." In *Collected Works of Warren S. McCulloch, Volume 1*, edited by Rook McCulloch, 21–49. Salinas: Intersystems Publications.

Müggenburg, Jan. 2016. "Trickkisten: Heinz von Foerster und der Zauber der Kybernetik." In *Trick 17: Mediengeschichten zwischen Zauberkunst und Wissenschaft*, edited by Sebastian Vehlken, Katja Müller-Helle, Jan Müggenburg, and Florian Sprenger, 59–84. Lüneburg: meson press.

Müggenburg, Jan, and Claus Pias. 2013. "Blöde Sklaven oder lebhafte Artefakte? Eine Debatte der 1960er." In *Automatismen: Selbst-Technologien*, edited by Hannelore Bublitz, Irina Kaldrack, Theo Röhle, and Mirna Zeman, 45–69. Munich: Fink.

Mumford, Lewis. 1967. *The Myth of the Machine: Technics and Human Development*. New York: Harcourt.

Newman, Max. 2006. "$\Delta\chi$-Method." In *Colossus: The Secrets of Bletchley Park's Codebreaking Computers*, edited by Jack Copeland, 386–90. New York: Oxford University Press.

Orwell, George. (1937) 2021. *The Road to Wigan Pier*. Oxford: Oxford University Press.

Petrick, Elizabeth R. 2020. "Building The Black Box: Cyberneticians and Complex Systems." *Science, Technology, & Human Values* 45 (4): 575–95.

Pickering, Andrew. 2002. "Cybernetics and The Mangle: Ashby, Beer and Pask." *Social Studies of Science* 32 (3): 413–37.

Price, David A. 2021. *Geniuses at War: Bletchley Park, Colossus, and The Dawn of The Digital Age*. New York: Penguin Random House.

Schneider, Ulrich Johannes. 2002. *Monadologie und andere metaphysische Schriften: Discours de métaphysique; Monadologie; Principes de la nature et de la grace fondès en raison*. Hamburg: Felix Meiner.

Shannon, Claude E. 1993. "A Mind-Reading (?) Machine." In *Claude E. Shannon: Collected Papers*, edited by Neil J. A. Sloane and Aaron D. Wyner, 688–90. New York: Wiley.

Strowger, Almon B. 1891. Automatic Telephone-Exchange. US Patent 447,918, filed March 12, 1889, and issued March 10, 1891.

Swade, Doron. 2019. "Forgotten Machines: The Need for a New Master Narrative." In *Exploring the Early Digital*, edited by Thomas Haigh, 41–68. Cham: Springer.

Tessmann, Oliver. 2008. "Collaborative Design Procedures for Architects and Engineers." PhD diss., University of Kassel.

Turing, Alan M. 1937. "On Computable Numbers, with an Application to the Entscheidungsproblem." *Proceedings of the London Mathematical Society* 42 (2): 230–65.

———. 1946. "Letter from Alan Turing to W. Ross Ashby." November 19, 1946. British Library Treasures Collection, MS 89153/26, British Library. https://www.bl.uk/collection-items/letter-from-alan-turing-to-w-ross-ashby.

———. 2001. "Visit to National Cash Register Corporation of Dayton, Ohio." *Cryptologia* 25 (1): 1–10.

Turner, Fred. 2006. *From Counterculture to Cyberculture: Stewart Brand, the Whole Earth Network, and the Rise of Digital Utopianism*. Chicago: University of Chicago Press.

Uribe, Ricardo B. 1991. *Tractatus Paradoxico-Philosophicus: A Philosophical Approach to Education, Red-Edition*. Urbana: self-published.

Vater, Christian. 2020. "Turings Maschine und Blacks Box: Mechanische Intelligenz nach dem Feedback." In *Black Boxes: Versiegelungskontexte und Öffnungsversuche*, edited by Eckhard Geitz, Christian Vater, and Silke Zimmer-Merkle, 323–50. Berlin: De Gruyter.

von Foerster, Heinz. 2003. *Understanding Understanding: Essays on Cybernetics and Cognition*. New York: Springer.

———.2014. *The Beginning of Heaven and Earth Has No Name: Seven Days with Second-Order Cybernetics*. New York: Fordham University Press.

von Hilgers, Philipp. 2010. "Ursprünge der Black Box." In *Rekursionen: Von Faltungen des Wissens*, edited by Ana Ofak and Philipp von Hilgers, 135–53. Munich: Fink.

———.2011. "The History of The Black Box: The Clash of a Thing and Its Concept." *Cultural Politics* 7 (1): 41–58.

Weber, Max. 1978. *Economy and Society: An Outline of Interpretive Sociology*. Berkeley: University of California Press.

Wiener, Norbert. (1948) 1961. *Cybernetics: Or Control and Communication in the Animal and the Machine, 2nd Edition*. Cambridge: MIT Press.

———.1989. *The Human Use of Human Beings: Cybernetics and Society*. London: Free Association Press.

Epilogue: The Cybernetic Revolution

Hans-Christian von Herrmann

In the spring of 1987, the colloquium "Materiality of Communication" took place at the Inter-University Center in Dubrovnik. Organized by the literary scholars K. Ludwig Pfeiffer and Hans Ulrich Gumbrecht, it was an international meeting which, due to Yugoslavia having been chosen as the location, also made encounters between the East and West possible. However, the subsequent publication by the German publishing house Suhrkamp (Gumbrecht and Pfeiffer 1988) was to have an impact primarily in the German-speaking world, where it contributed significantly to the establishment of media-theoretical approaches in the humanities and their new self-definition as cultural sciences. Among the texts contained in this over-900-page volume is Friedrich Kittler's lecture "*Signal-to-Noise Ratio*," whose considerations bring together Claude E. Shannon's mathematical theory of communication, Norbert Wiener's statistical automaton theory, and Jacques Lacan's structural psychoanalysis. The last sentence in that document sums up Kittler's approach as follows: "An unoccupied space has emerged, where one might substitute the practice of interception for the theory of reception, and polemics for hermeneutics. Indeed, one might inaugurate *hermenautics*—a pilot's understanding of signals, whether they stem from gods, machines, or sources of noise." (Kittler 2018 [1988], 360). What is formulated here as the pilot's knowledge of technical communication processes—or "cybernetics"—marks a historical caesura that allows engineering knowledge to take the place of scriptural scholarship. The literary scholar Marshall McLuhan had already made a similar move around 1960 with his formula of the "end of the Gutenberg galaxy"—"the Gutenberg galaxy is being eclipsed by the constellation of Marconi" (McLuhan [1969] 1997, 234)—but in doing so he argued largely in terms of (media) aesthetics. The turn to the "materiality of communication" was then to trigger a foundational crisis in the German tradition of the humanities, followed by the attempt to find new foundations such as the concept of media, which McLuhan had already used but had hardly made explicit.

After cybernetics had initially been appropriated, rather than just thematized from the side of the humanities—as in Friedrich Kittler's 1987 lecture, following the intention to technicize its thinking—a historical interest in the beginnings of cybernetic thinking emerged in the 1990s (Galison 1994; Segal 2001; Pickering 2002), which was soon taken up in German-speaking media culture studies (Pias 2004; Hagner and Hörl 2008). Among other things, this brought to light that philosophical and literary reactions to cybernetics could already be found in the 1950s and 1960s. For example, in 1951, Max Bense, professor of philosophy of science at the Technische Hochschule Stuttgart, stated in a commentary on Norbert Wiener's 1948 book *Cybernetics: Or Control and Communication in the Animal and the Machine* (Wiener 1948):

> The cybernetic extension of modern technology means its extension under the skin of the world; technology can no longer be considered in any way isolated (objectified) from the world process and its sociological, ideological, and vital phases. It involves everything, it has taken on an intensified consuming character. Literature, art, music take on its features. (Bense 1998, 436)[1]

Therefore, Bense saw in cybernetics not only a technological, but also an anthropological caesura:

> Under the impression of a penetration of technical phenomena into the deeper layers of human relations of being, as cybernetic machines have made obvious, one is forced to see technology as a possible solution to that anthropologically determinable disproportion [between man and nature]. Through technology, man creates for himself

---

1   All quotes from sources in German translated by the author.

an environment appropriate to his dual role as a natural and spiritual being. (Bense 1998, 446)

When a "focus on cybernetics" was established at the Technische Universität Berlin in 1963, as one of several interdisciplinary and interfaculty research clusters, the Faculty of Philosophy was also involved. Within this framework, in November 1964 the linguist Klaus Baumgärtner, research assistant at Walter Höllerer's Institute for Language in the Technical Age, gave a lecture on "Cybernetic Language Models." At the same time, the Faculty of Philosophy was pursuing the plan to establish a chair for "Humanistic Foundations of Cybernetics and Automation" (Walter Höllerer Estate). In the mid-1950s, Jacques Lacan, in his Paris Seminars, saw cybernetics as the culmination of a "conjectural" rationality (Lacan [1972] 1991, 375)—in the sense of Jacob Bernoulli's *Ars conjectandi*—that, in its beginnings, went back to the early modern period and required a redefinition of human existence under the sign of a chance that had become universal.

In his 1832 treatise *On War* (*Vom Kriege*), Carl von Clausewitz had used the physical concept of "friction" to refer to the fact that modern war, with its complex processes organized in space and time, is "everywhere in contact with chance" and therefore produces "phenomena" that "cannot be calculated at all" (Clausewitz [1832] 1991, 262). With thermodynamics and its statistical models, however, the "mathematical formalization of the Chaos of old" (Kittler 2018 [1988], 357) was soon to move onto the scientific agenda. It was the frictions or unpredictabilities of World War II that stood at the beginning of cybernetics as an interdisciplinary research field, thus establishing the significance of feedback.

In January 1943, physiologist Arturo Rosenblueth, mathematician Norbert Wiener, and electrical engineer Julian Bigelow published an essay in the journal *Philosophy of Science* introducing their concept of feedback as a new behavioral science category. The appearance of the text in the wartime year of 1943 had a very concrete background: the attempts of Wiener and Bigelow to develop a feedback anti-aircraft predictor, which should improve the efficiency of the Allied air defense. Of course, the text does not speak of this activity in the context of the US military, but instead speaks of cats and mice, of snakes, frogs, and flies, of stones thrown at moving targets, and, last but not least, of machines capable of detecting a light source and moving toward it. The methodological point of the three authors is that they summarize these very different processes under a common term; namely, that of purposeful and teleological behavior. This is explicitly not the assumption of an equality of essence, but an observation and description procedure, which calls itself behavioristic and by which living beings and machines were entering into a new relationship of close proximity. In this process, the concept of behavior loses all psychological connotations by referring quite generally to the study of both animate and inanimate objects in relation to their environment.

> Given any object, relatively abstracted from its surroundings for study, the behavioristic approach consists in the examination of the output of the object and of the relations of this output to the input. By output is meant any change produced in the surroundings by the object. By input, conversely, is meant any event external to the object that modifies this object in any manner. (Rosenblueth, Wiener, and Bigelow 1943, 18)

Thus, behavior in the sense used by Rosenblueth, Wiener, and Bigelow does not imply any assumptions about the nature of the observed objects, but describes only a relation—input-output—completely independent of any functional aspects. At the same time, a profound change in the meaning of technology becomes apparent, since we are now dealing with machines that show teleological behavior on the basis of negative feedback, or, as one can also say, operate between their past, present, and future.

Cybernetics, which was formed in the post-war years, initially in
the USA as an interdisciplinary research program of life sciences,
engineering, and social sciences, can be seen as an attempt to
gain a new understanding of technology and a new view of its
relation to human beings beyond the dispute between vitalism
and mechanism, based on the purposeful behavior of new
machines open to their environment. As a systems theory encom-
passing both machines and living beings, it took up the mathematical neuron model of Warren McCulloch and Walter Pitts,
the game theory of John von Neumann and Oskar Morgenstern,
and the information theory of Claude E. Shannon, in addition
to control engineering. Thus, as the German anthropologist
Arnold Gehlen stated in 1957, "technology ... advanced to the
center of man's interpretation of the world and thus also of his
conception of himself" (Gehlen 1957, 14), because the new non-
deterministic technical systems transferred their probabilistic
mode of operation to the understanding of human activity in all
its dimensions.

From the point of view of a history of knowledge, what character-
izes the cybernetic notion of behavior first formulated by Rosenblueth, Wiener, and Bigelow in 1943, is its ability to be adaptable
to very different disciplines and to trigger—in Thomas Kuhn's
sense—revolutions in them, by establishing new paradigms.
What is striking in any case, is the tremendous productivity that
cybernetic descriptive methods were able to unleash, and whose
scope seemed to have almost no limits in the entire spectrum;
from elementary laboratory research to cosmological specu-
lation. The success of cybernetics as a new order of knowledge
in a postwar era that saw itself as a "technical age" (Gehlen 1957;
Walter Höllerer Estate) was not limited to the realm of scientific
methods, but also encompassed new concepts of organization
and control in economics, politics, and pedagogy. The cybernetic
concept of "behavior"—like the concepts of "information" and
"system"—was assigned the function of a linguistic shifter
that could be moved across disciplinary boundaries, could be

 applied to the most diverse phenomena, and through which technology and society were at the same time brought ever closer together. This also made it possible not only to speak of machine or artificial intelligence as a matter of course, but also to tackle a cybernetization of art and aesthetics, which, although it hardly had anything to do with the initial research program of cybernetics, nevertheless allowed its machine-like notion of behavior to penetrate into a core area of modern anthropology. For example, against the backdrop of May 1968 in Paris, the French artist Nicolas Schöffer conceived the utopia of a "cybernetic city" in which individual and social life would be liberated to universal controllability. "According to Schöffer, the artist is the creator, or rather the programmer, of effects brought about through technologically controlled environments which are able to condition—and manipulate—human behavior and specific activities" (Darò 2014, 9).

Wiener's *Cybernetics* was published in Paris in 1948, whereupon *Le Monde* commissioned the Dominican monk Dominique Dubarle to review it. For him, the new cybernetic machines possessed the threatening potential to give rise to entirely new forms of political rule, and to transform themselves into machines *à gouverner*.

> At all events, human realities do not admit sharp and certain determination, as numerical data of computation do. They only admit the determination of their probable values. A machine to treat these processes, and the problems which they put, must therefore undertake the sort of probabilistic, rather than deterministic thought, such as is exhibited for example in modern computing machines. (Wiener 1954, 179)

Wiener took up Dubarle's review in his book *The Human Use of Human Beings* ([1950] 1954), but took the view that the range of variation in human behavior could not ultimately be handled by machine predictions. Today we are dealing with a completely different situation in terms of computing capacity, with artificial neural networks learning their predictive capabilities on large amounts of data. This includes the observation that the "cybernetic revolution" (Schölkopf 2018), which began in the 1940s with the formulation of a new notion of behavior, now provides in many respects the knowledge with which highly technological societies describe and organize themselves as complex systems.

References

Bense, Max. (1951) 1998. "Kybernetik oder Die Metatechnik einer Maschine." In *Ausgewählte Schriften, Volume 2: Philosophie der Mathematik, Naturwissenschaft und Technik*, 429–46. Stuttgart/Weimar: Metzler Verlag.

Clausewitz, Carl von. (1832) 1991. *Vom Kriege*. Bonn: Dümmlers.

Darò, Carlotta. 2014. "Nicolas Schöffer and the Cybernetic City." *AA Files* 69 (2014): 3–11.

Gumbrecht, Hans Ulrich, and K. Ludwig Pfeiffer, eds. 1988. *Materialität der Kommunikation*. Frankfurt am Main: Suhrkamp Verlag.

Galison, Peter. 1994. "The Ontology of the Enemy: Norbert Wiener and the Cybernetic Vision." *Critical Inquiry* 21 (1): 228–66.

Gehlen, Arnold. 1957. Die Seele im technischen Zeitalter. Sozialpsychologische Probleme in der industriellen Gesellschaft. Reinbek: Rowohlt Verlag.

Hagner, Michael, and Erich Hörl, eds. 2008. *Die Transformation des Humanen: Beiträge zur Kulturgeschichte der Kybernetik*. Frankfurt am Main: Suhrkamp Verlag.

Kittler, Friedrich. 2018 [1988]. "Signal-to-Noise Ratio." In *Disruption in the Arts: Textual, Visual, and Performative Strategies for Analyzing Societal Self-Descriptions*, edited by Lars Koch, Tobias Nanz, and Johannes Pause, 347–61. Berlin, Boston: De Gruyter, 2018. https://doi.org/10.1515/9783110580082.

Lacan, Jacques. (1972) 1991. *Das Seminar Buch II (1954–1955): Das Ich in der Theorie Freunds und in der Technik der Psychoanalyse, 2nd Edition*. Weinheim/Berlin: Quadriga.

Literaturarchiv Sulzbach-Rosenberg, Walter Höllerer Estate.

McLuhan, Marshall. (1969) 1997. "Marshall McLuhan—A Candid Conversation with the High Priest of Popcult and Metaphysician of Media (Playboy interview)." In *Essential McLuhan*, edited by Eric McLuhan and Frank Zingrone, 222–60. London: Routledge.

Pias, Claus. 2004. *Cybernetics—Kybernetik: The Macy-Conferences 1946–1953. Essays & Dokumente*. Zürich/Berlin: Diaphanes.

Pickering, Andrew. 2002. "Cybernetics and the Mangle: Ashby, Beer and Pask." *Social Studies of Science* 32 (3): 413–37.

Rosenblueth, Arturo, Norbert Wiener, and Julian Bigelow. 1943. "Behavior, Purpose and Teleology." *Philosophy of Science* 10 (1): 18–24.

Schölkopf, Bernhard. 2018. "Kybernetische Revolution: Künstliche Intelligenz wird Leben und Arbeiten so stark ändern wie einst Elektrizität. Europa braucht

202   dafür die besten Köpfe." *Süddeutsche Zeitung*, March 16, 2018. https://www.sueddeutsche.de/politik/aussenansicht-kybernetische-revolution-1.3907249.

Segal, Jérôme. 2001. "Kybernetik in der DDR: Begegnung mit der marxistischen Ideologie." *Dresdener Beiträge zur Geschichte der Technikwissenschaften* 27 (2001): 47–75.

Wiener, Norbert. 1948. *Cybernetics: Or Control and Communication in the Animal and the Machine*. Paris, Cambridge, and New York: Hermann & Cie. Editeurs, The Technology Press, John Wiley & Sons.

———. (1950) 1954. *The Human Use of Human Beings: Cybernetics and Society, 2nd Edition*. New York: Da Capo Press.

Authors

Andrei Cretu is a teaching assistant professor in the Department of Slavic and East European Languages at The Ohio State University and a recipient of the American Society for Cybernetics' Heinz von Foerster Award. His research focuses on communication theory and the mathematical modeling of language.

Wolfgang Ernst is chair of Media Theories at Humboldt-Universität zu Berlin. His research covers media archaeology as method, theory of technical storage, technologies of cultural transmission, micro-temporal media aesthetics, critique of history as master discourse of cultural and technological time, and sound analysis from a media-epistemological perspective.

Thomas Fischer is a professor at the School of Design at the Southern University of Science and Technology, a fellow of the Design Research Society, and recipient of the American Society for Cybernetics' Warren McCulloch Award. His research focuses on design computing, design cybernetics, and digital media.

Diego Gómez-Venegas is a PhD candidate at the Institute of Musicology and Media Sciences (Media Sciences section) of Humboldt-Universität zu Berlin. His work focuses on the media-archaeo-genealogical traces of cybernetics and its links to our contemporary condition.

Hans-Christian von Herrmann holds the chair of Literary Studies (Literature and Science) at Technische Universität Berlin. His work focuses on the change in literary culture in the age of cybernetization, practices of automation in the arts since the late 19th century, and the effects of planetarization associated with modern technology.

204 **Stefan Höltgen** (PhD, ScD) is scholar for media science at University of Bonn. He researches and teaches media and computer archaeology, and works as scientific advisor for the Oldenburg Computer Museum.

Rolf F. Nohr is professor of Media Aesthetics and Media Culture at HBK Braunschweig, and an external affiliate at the College of Humanities of University of Arizona. His work focuses on media evidence processes, game studies and instantaneous images.

Eva Schauerte is a media and cultural historian with a focus on media history of computer democracy. In the past she held research positions at the Institute for Media Culture Studies at Albert-Ludwigs-University Freiburg (2011–2016), and at IKKM (2016–2020). Currently, she works for the Senate Chancellery of Bremen.

Isabell Schrickel is a PhD candidate at the Center for Global Sustainability and Cultural Transformation (Leuphana University / Arizona State University). Isabell was visiting fellow at Harvard's Department of the History of Science and at IKKM. Her work historicizes environmental sciences, modeling and simulation, and the evolution of sustainability thinking.

Sebastian Vehlken is professor of Knowledge Processes and Digital Media at Universität Oldenburg, and head of the program area Ships as Knowledge Repositories at the German Maritime Museum/Leibniz-Institute for Maritime History. His research interests include the media history of computer simulation, media of futurology, and oceans as knowledge spaces.